Lib 15

Kent Libraries & Archives

Reference Collection

91000

C153551127

e.explore

Weather

KENT
LIBRARIES & ARCHIVES
C153551127

LONDON, NEW YORK, MELBOURNE,
MUNICH, and DELHI

Project Editor Susan Malyan
Weblink Editors Roger Brownlie, Niki Foreman, Clare Lister

Senior Editor Claire Nottage
Managing Editor Linda Esposito

Digital Development Manager Fergus Day
DTP Co-ordinators Siu Chan, Andy Hilliard

Jacket Copywriter Adam Powley
Jacket Editor Mariza O'Keeffe

Publishing Managers Andrew Macintyre, Caroline Buckingham

Consultant Dr Roger Brugge, University of Reading

Project Art Editor Marilou Prokopiou
Designers Spencer Holbrook, Philip Letsu, Jane Thomas
Illustrator John Plumer

Senior Art Editor Jim Green
Managing Art Editor Diane Thistlethwaite

Picture Research Liz Moore
Picture Librarians Rose Horridge, Claire Bowers

Production Erica Rosen
Jacket Designer Neal Cobourne

Cartography Ed Merritt, Simon Mumford

First published in Great Britain in 2007
by Dorling Kindersley Limited, 80 Strand, London WC2R 0RL

Penguin Group

Copyright © 2007 Dorling Kindersley Limited

Google™ is a trademark of Google Technology Inc.

2 4 6 8 10 9 7 5 3 1

All rights reserved. No part of this publication may be reproduced, stored in a retrieval system, or transmitted in any form or by any means, electronic, mechanical, photocopying, recording, or otherwise, without the prior written permission of the copyright owner.

A CIP catalogue for this book is available from the British Library.

ISBN-13: 978-1-40531-346-9
ISBN-10: 1-4053-1346-3

Colour reproduction by Colourscan, Singapore
Printed in China by Toppan Printing Co. (Shenzen) Ltd.

Discover more at
www.dk.com

e.explore

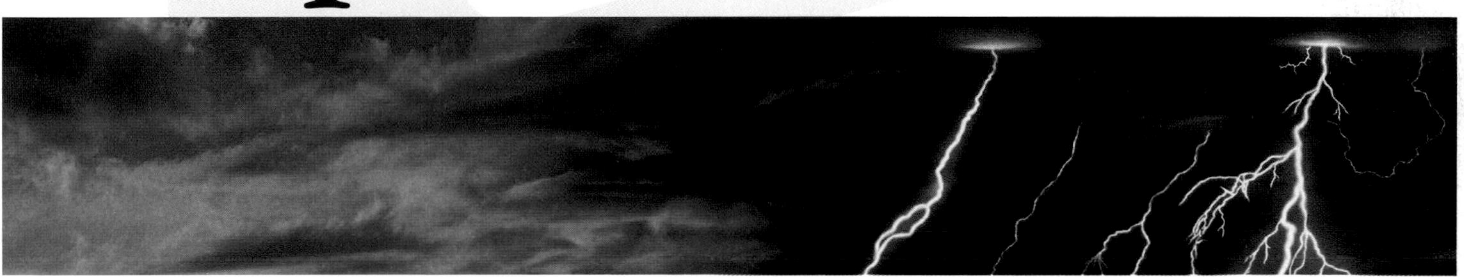

Weather

Written by John Woodward

Google™

CONTENTS

How to use the e.explore website

e.explore Weather has its own website, created by DK and Google™. When you look up a subject in the book, the article gives you key facts and displays a keyword that links you to extra information online. Just follow these easy steps.

http://www.weather.dke-explore.com

Enter this website address...

2 Find the keyword in the book...

You can use only the keywords from the book to search on our website for the specially selected DK/Google links.

Enter the keyword...

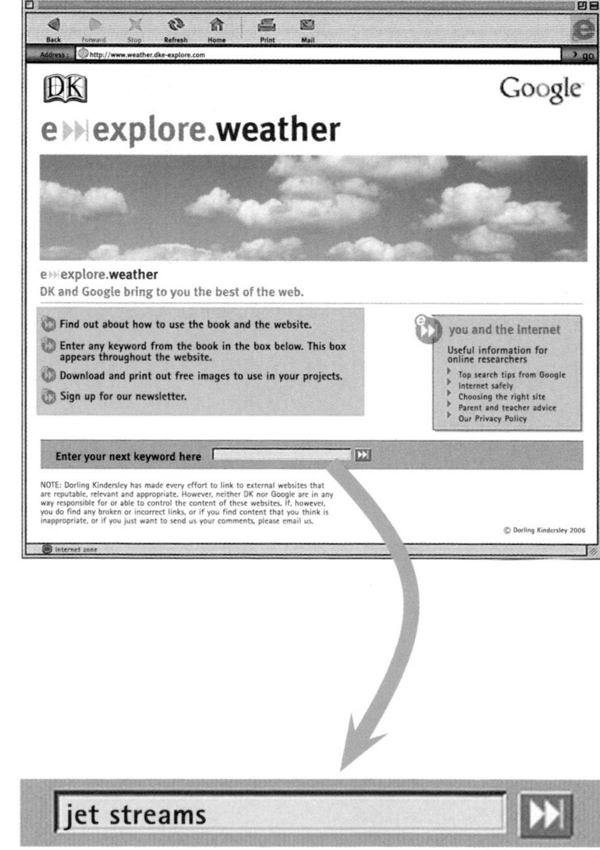

Be safe while you are online:

- Always get permission from an adult before connecting to the internet.
- Never give out personal information about yourself.
- Never arrange to meet someone you have talked to online.
- If a site asks you to log in with your name or email address, ask permission from an adult first.
- Do not reply to emails from strangers – tell an adult.

Parents: Dorling Kindersley actively and regularly reviews and updates the links. However, content may change. Dorling Kindersley is not responsible for any site but its own. We recommend that children are supervised while online, that they do not use Chat Rooms, and that filtering software is used to block unsuitable material.

Click on your chosen link...

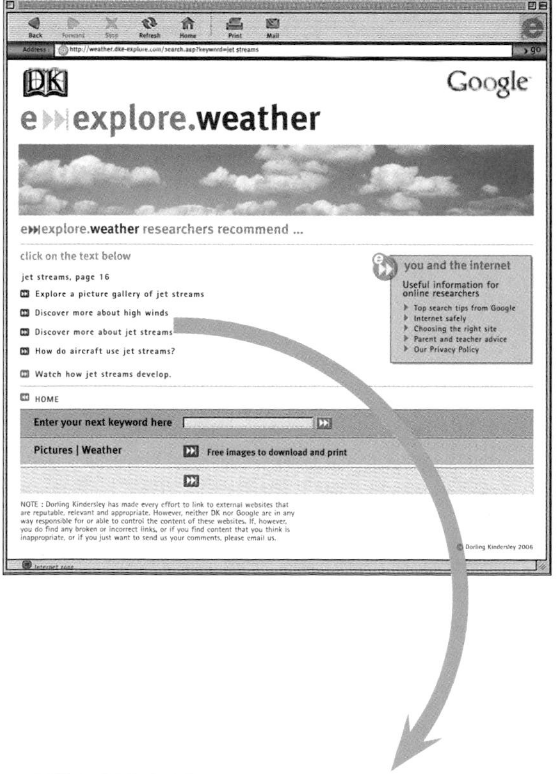

Discover more about jet streams

Links include animations, videos, sound buttons, virtual tours, interactive quizzes, databases, timelines, and realtime reports.

Download fantastic pictures...

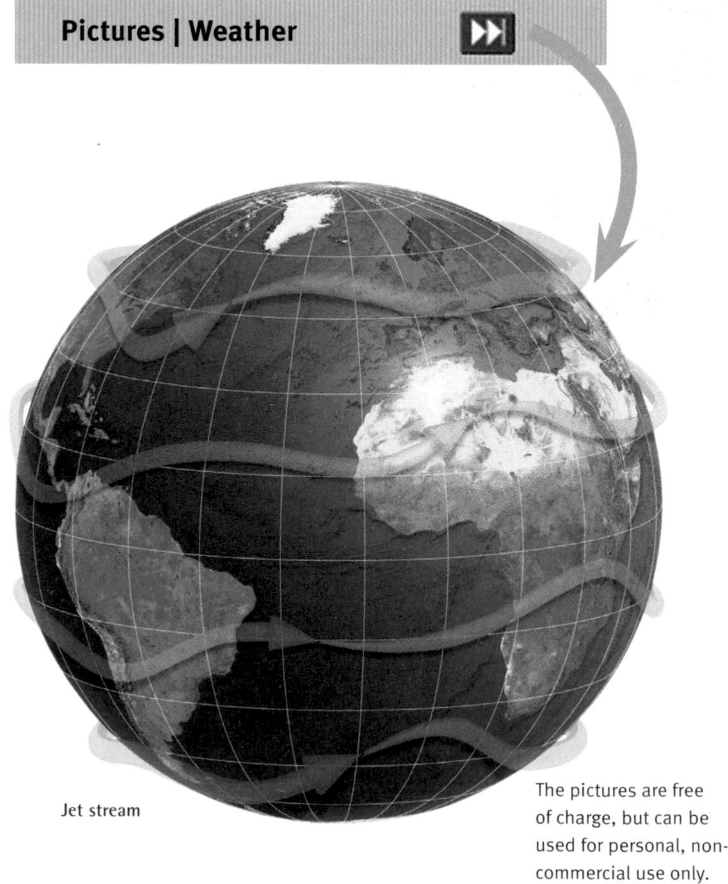

The pictures are free of charge, but can be used for personal, non-commercial use only.

Go back to the book for your next subject...

WEATHER AND CLIMATE

We are all interested in the weather. We wonder if today is going to be hot or cold, wet or dry. We want to know what to wear, and if it is a good day to go to the beach. Some people have to know about the weather to make a living, or even to survive. A serious storm can wreck a farmer's crop or sink a fishing boat. At its worst, extreme weather can even destroy entire cities and cause terrible famines, so the weather has a big influence on all our lives.

CLIMATE

DRY AND DUSTY
The average weather in any place is known as its climate. Climates are fairly predictable, although they can change gradually over the years. For example, somewhere with a desert climate, like the Sahara, is always relatively dry and barren. There may be occasional rainstorms, but the average annual rainfall is never enough to make up for all the moisture that evaporates into the air.

LUSH AND GREEN
Regions near the sea tend to get a lot of rain. So although the weather may be warm and dry in summer, the overall climate is relatively damp. The influence of the sea often stops the weather becoming very icy in winter, so these regions never get as cold as similar places in the middle of big continents. Plants grow well in these mild "maritime" climates, creating lush, green landscapes.

▲ RAIN STOPS PLAY
The weather is a complex mixture of atmospheric effects, including temperature, amount of cloud, wind, and rain. These things are always changing – although some regions have more changeable weather than others. Places like Britain are notorious for the way the weather keeps changing, so outdoor events such as tennis tournaments are often interrupted by rain. But other places, such as California, enjoy predictable sunshine all summer.

Lightning is uncontrollable – we do not know where it will strike

UNCONTROLLABLE FORCES ►
The weather is beyond our control. We can try to understand and predict it, but we cannot make it do what we want. We can only try to protect ourselves from violent weather events, and learn to predict when they may strike. Sometimes the things we do can influence the weather. Air pollution, for example, creates smogs and haze, and may be causing global climate change. But the consequences of this change are also out of our control.

◄ THE MOVING ATMOSPHERE
Our weather is caused by air currents in the atmosphere – the layer of gas that surrounds the Earth. The way the atmosphere moves is extremely complicated, but it does follow patterns that we understand. This makes it possible to forecast the weather. But the exact movements of the atmosphere are still difficult to predict accurately. Forecasters may know that a rainstorm is coming, for example, but they could not say exactly where and when it will strike.

NORMAL WEATHER ►
The difference between normal and extreme weather depends on where you are. Some places in the world regularly get weather that people living elsewhere would consider extreme. Yet since it is typical of the local climate, the local people consider it normal. Torrential rain is perfectly normal in central Java, for example, which has a thunderstorm almost every day. The same weather would make the news if it occurred in Sydney, Australia, which has a relatively dry climate.

PREDICTING THE WEATHER

Weather forecasting is improving all the time, thanks to new technology and a better understanding of the way the weather works. Information collected by satellites and automatic weather stations is fed into powerful computers to provide a detailed, up-to-date picture of the weather worldwide. The computers then use this data to predict how the weather is likely to develop over the next few days. Satellites can even give us a view of the weather from space, such as this image of a hurricane threatening the east coast of the USA.

◄ EXTREME WEATHER
Some weather is so extreme that no one would call it normal. Hurricanes are part of the climate in some parts of the world, such as the Caribbean, but they rarely strike in exactly the same place twice. So when hurricanes do sweep in from the ocean, they often hit islands and cities that are not prepared to withstand them. This is Cancun in Mexico after Hurricane Wilma swept through the city in October 2005, flattening buildings and bringing down power lines.

▼ CLIMATE THREAT
For much of history, people have been used to local climates that do not alter much. There may have been droughts, storms, or frosts, but we have always known that the weather would soon return to normal. But now the threat of drastic climate change has destroyed this comforting certainty. Each unusual weather event is now seen as a possible sign of a chaotic, unpredictable future. As a result, exploring the weather is more vital than ever.

THE EARTH IN SPACE

The world's weather is shaped by our planet's size and its position in space. Earth is one of nine major planets circling around the star that we call the Sun. Most of the outer planets are huge balls of gas with small rocky cores, but Earth is one of four small inner planets that are mostly made of rock. Earth is close enough to the Sun to be relatively warm, so oceans of water can exist on its surface, and it has an atmosphere. Heat from the Sun sets Earth's water and atmosphere in motion, and this causes our weather.

▲ GRAVITY
Earth was formed from iron-rich meteorite rock that clumped together to form a rocky sphere. The energy of the meteorite impacts melted the rock and allowed most of the iron to collect at the Earth's core. The weight of the core gives Earth enough gravity to hold on to its atmosphere.

THE SOLAR SYSTEM ▲
Our Solar System is made up of the Sun and its nine planets. The four inner, rocky planets – Mercury, Venus, Earth, and Mars – are separated from the other five planets by a broad band of orbiting rocky debris, called the asteroid belt. The planets were formed from similar rocky debris, which once orbited the Sun in a much broader band, like a spinning disc. This is why all the major planets orbit in the same plane, apart from the small planet Pluto, which probably had a different origin. Each planet travels in an ellipse (oval) shaped orbit, and the further it is from the Sun, the longer a planet takes to complete one orbit. Earth takes one year to travel right round the Sun.

THE PLANETS

PLANET NAME	*DISTANCE FROM THE SUN*
1 Mercury	58 m km (36 m miles)
2 Venus	108 m km (67 m miles)
3 Earth	150 m km (93 m miles)
4 Mars	228 m km (142 m miles)
5 Jupiter	778 m km (486 m miles)
6 Saturn	1,429 m km (893 m miles)
7 Uranus	2,870 m km (1,794 m miles)
8 Neptune	4,504 m km (2,815 m miles)
9 Pluto	5,913 m km (3,696 m miles)

▲ WATER
Earth is the only planet in the Solar System where water can exist in all three states – as a solid (ice), a liquid (water), or a gas (water vapour). This allows clouds and rain to be formed from ocean water. When water changes from one state to another it absorbs or releases energy, in a form known as latent heat. This energy helps to drive our planet's weather systems.

OTHER PLANETS IN THE SOLAR SYSTEM

MERCURY
The smallest of the inner planets, and closest to the Sun, Mercury has no insulating atmosphere and no weather. Its surface is exposed to the full glare of the Sun and reaches a daytime temperature of 400°C (750°F). But at night, the surface temperature falls to –175°C (–283°F) as heat escapes into space.

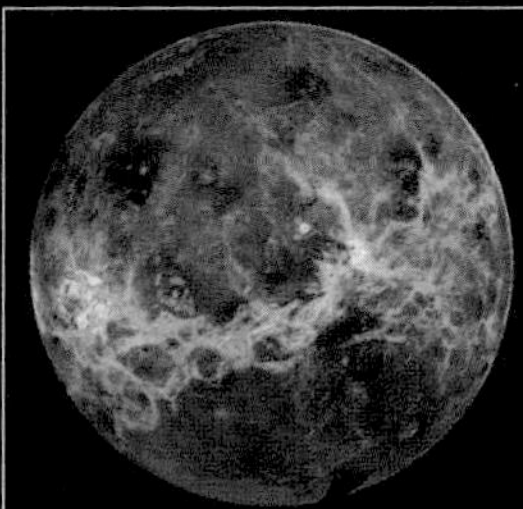

VENUS
Roughly the same size as Earth, the planet Venus has a thick atmosphere that is 96.4 per cent carbon dioxide. This atmosphere acts like a blanket around the planet, stopping heat escaping into space. As a result, the temperature on the surface of Venus is about 500°C (930°F) – hot enough to melt lead.

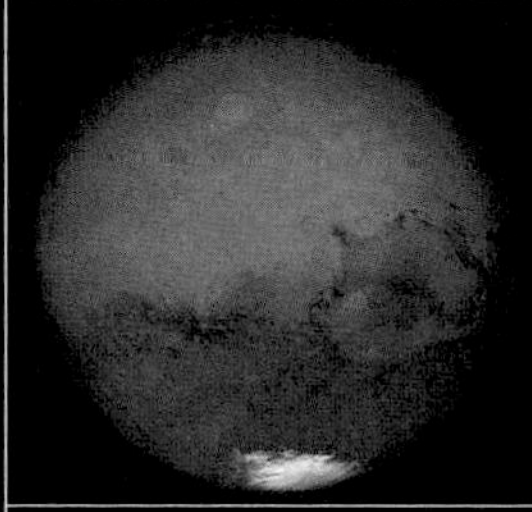

MARS
Mars is more like Earth than any of the other planets, but since it is smaller it has less gravity and a thinner atmosphere. Mars is also further away from the Sun, and the temperature of its warmest region rises to only about 10°C (50°F). At night, the temperature regularly drops below –140°C (–220°F).

JUPITER
Jupiter is the largest planet in the Solar System. Its diameter is one-tenth of the diameter of the Sun. But most of Jupiter's immense volume is a huge mass of swirling gas. About 90 per cent of this is hydrogen, the lightest of all the gases. The temperature at the top of Jupiter's clouds is about -145°C (-230°F).

LIFE ON EARTH

The presence of water on Earth has enabled life to exist and to evolve into a wonderful variety of forms, from the simplest microbes to giant trees and beautiful animals. The diversity of life on Earth is partly a result of our planet's range of weather patterns and climates. But the presence of living things can also affect the atmosphere and the local weather. For example, all the oxygen in our atmosphere was originally released by living things.

Breathing equipment

Astronauts can leap across the Moon's surface because of its low gravity

◄ THE MOON
Earth has its own orbiting body – the Moon. It was probably formed from a cloud of dust blasted off Earth by a planetary collision, early in the history of the Solar System. Since most of the dust came from Earth's rocky mantle, and not from its iron core, the Moon contains a smaller percentage of iron than Earth. This makes it relatively light, with little gravity. But its low gravity means that the Moon has no atmosphere, and so it has no weather.

THE ATMOSPHERE

Earth is covered by a layer of air that forms its atmosphere. By day, the atmosphere protects the Earth's surface from the full glare of the Sun and absorbs damaging ultraviolet radiation. At night, it stops heat from escaping into space. The flow of air in the lower levels of the atmosphere moves heat around the globe, helping to reduce extremes of heat and cold. This airflow is also responsible for the world's weather.

THIN AIR

Most of the gases in the atmosphere are concentrated in its lowest layer, the troposphere, so the density of air decreases with altitude. If you were to travel just 10 km (6 miles) upwards, which is not far by the standards of overland journeys, you would enter a realm where there is barely enough air to keep you alive. This is why mountaineers climbing Himalayan peaks, such as Mount Everest, often have to wear breathing apparatus.

▼ A SHALLOW LAYER
The atmosphere is a relatively shallow layer of air that thins out rapidly at high altitude. Photographs taken from spacecraft show its blue glow fading into the airless darkness of deep space. Clouds and weather only occur in the lowest level of the atmosphere, called the troposphere.

AIR COMPOSITION

COMPONENTS	PERCENTAGE
Nitrogen	78%
Oxygen	20%
Argon	1%
Carbon dioxide	0.04%
Other gases	up to 1%

▲ GAS MIXTURE
The air we breathe is a mixture of gases. Its two main ingredients are nitrogen and oxygen. Carbon dioxide, which is so vital to life, accounts for just a small fraction of the air. The rest consists primarily of argon, neon, helium, ozone, hydrogen, and krypton, with tiny amounts of other gases.

Thermosphere gradually thins out until there are no air molecules left

Mesopause is the boundary between the mesosphere and the thermosphere

Stratopause is the boundary between the stratosphere and the mesosphere

Tropopause is the boundary between the troposphere and the stratosphere

Thermosphere 87 km (54 miles) upwards

Mesosphere 50–87 km (31–54 miles)

Stratosphere 18–50 km (11–31 miles)

Troposphere 0–18 km (0–11 miles)

Sea level

In the thermosphere air becomes hotter as height increases

In the mesosphere air becomes cooler as the altitude increases

In the stratosphere the temperature rises with altitude, as UV radiation is absorbed by ozone

In the troposphere the air temperature falls as the altitude increases

▲ LAYERS

The atmosphere consists of several deep layers. The lowest layer is the troposphere, which contains most of the gas in the atmosphere, and is where all our weather occurs. Above the troposphere lies the stratosphere, which contains the ozone layer, and then the mesosphere. Beyond this is the thermosphere, which has no definite upper limit, but fades away into the vacuum of space.

▲ ATMOSPHERIC BOUNDARIES

The boundary between two layers in the atmosphere is set by a temperature inversion – a point at which, instead of falling with altitude, the temperature starts to rise (or the other way round). These temperature inversions stop air moving freely between the layers.

▲ BURNING METEORS

The gas density in the upper atmosphere is very low, but there is enough of it to present a barrier to meteors. As they fall towards Earth, they are heated by friction and small ones burn out as shooting stars.

▲ CAPPING THE WEATHER

Warm, moist air may rise towards the stratosphere, forming deep cumulonimbus clouds. But the temperature inversion at the tropopause stops the air rising any further, so it tends to spread out sideways instead. So the tropopause acts like a lid on the world's weather.

OXYGEN PRODUCERS

Much of the oxygen in the atmosphere was made by microscopic organisms that lived over 2 billion years ago. They resembled the cyanobacteria colonies still found in the waters of Shark Bay in Australia. These bacteria use the energy of sunlight to make sugar from carbon dioxide and water, in a process that releases oxygen.

SOLAR ENERGY

Inside the Sun, hydrogen gas is constantly being turned into helium. This process releases energy, which radiates out into space. Only a tiny fraction of this energy reaches Earth, but it is enough to light our planet and keep it warm. And it is heat from the Sun that keeps the atmosphere moving and causes our weather.

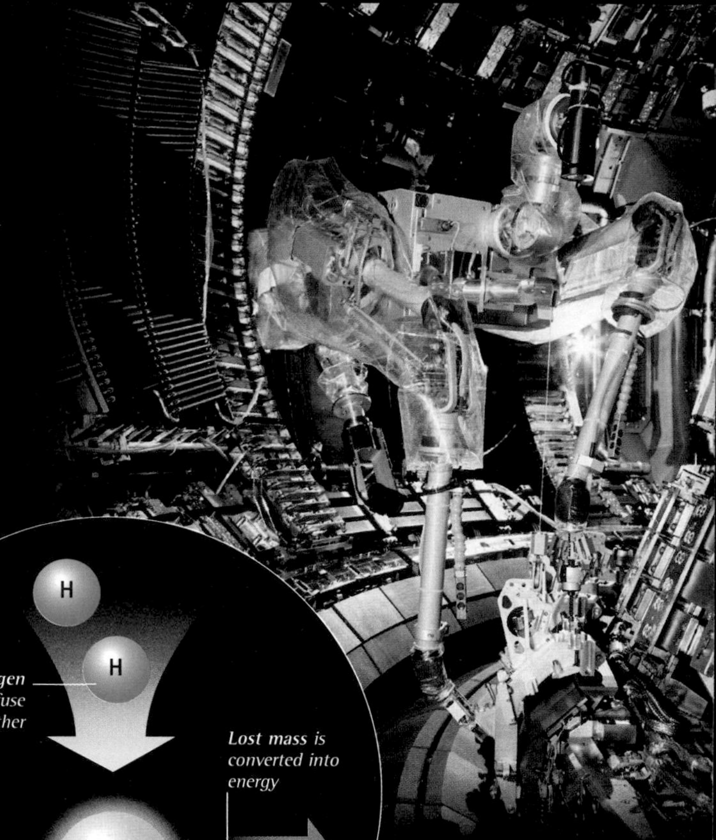

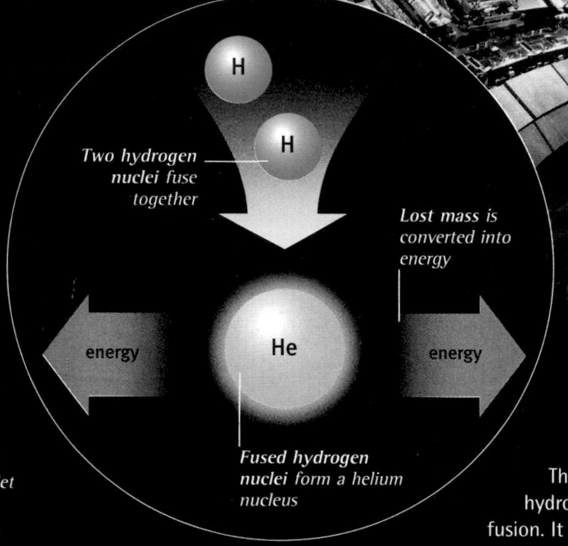

e solar energy

Gamma-rays have the shortest wavelength

X-rays lie just beyond the ultraviolet

Ultraviolet radiation is invisible, but a major part of the solar energy spectrum

Sunlight is a combination of all the colours of the visible spectrum

Infrared solar radiation is invisible, but can be felt as heat

Microwaves lie between the wavelengths of infrared and radiowaves

Radiowaves are the longest waves in the electromagnetic spectrum

H

H

Two hydrogen nuclei fuse together

Lost mass is converted into energy

energy

He

energy

Fused hydrogen nuclei form a helium nucleus

▲ NUCLEAR FUSION
The process by which the Sun turns hydrogen into helium is called nuclear fusion. It takes two hydrogen nuclei, fused together under conditions of extreme heat and pressure, to create one helium nucleus. But each helium nucleus weighs slightly less than two hydrogen nuclei, so some mass is lost. This lost mass is converted into energy, in the form of electromagnetic radiation. Here on Earth, scientists are trying to harness nuclear fusion as a source of energy, using experimental fusion reactors such as the one shown above.

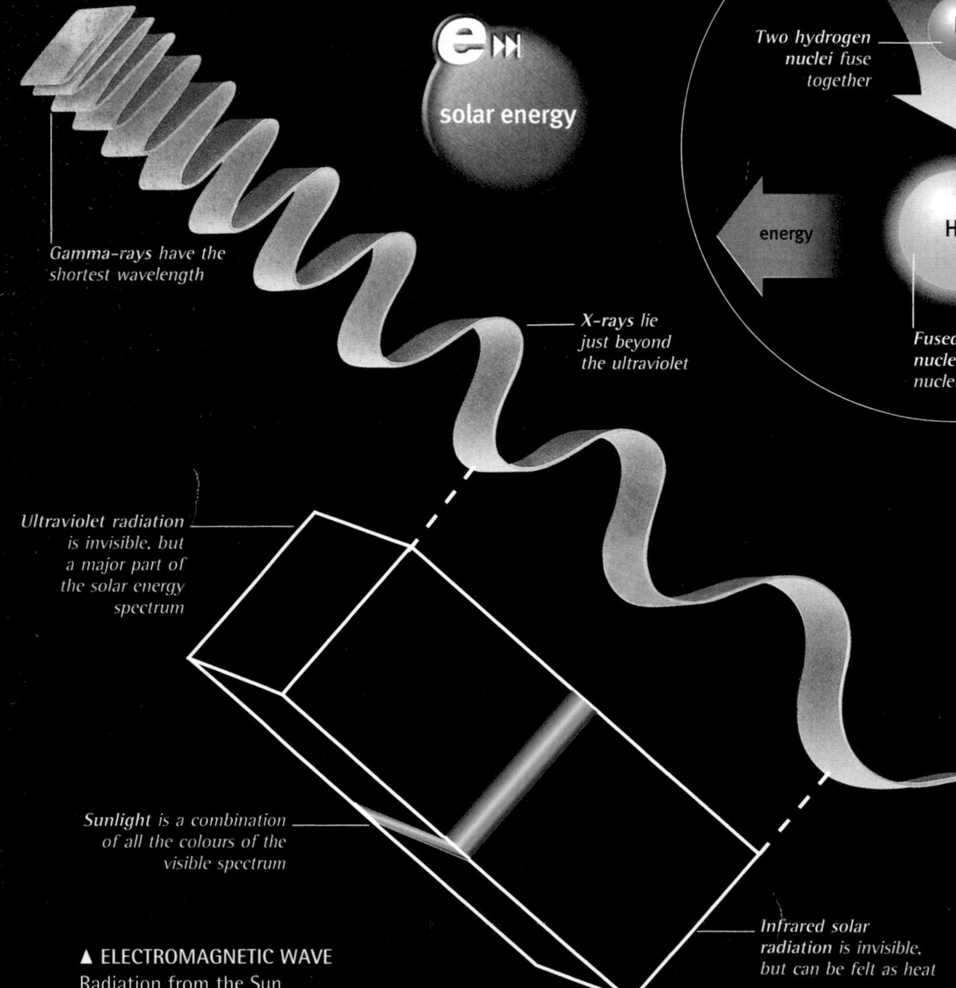

▲ ELECTROMAGNETIC WAVE
Radiation from the Sun includes all the wavelengths of the electromagnetic spectrum, from very short-wave gamma-rays to very long radiowaves. But 99.9 per cent of solar radiation lies in the range from ultraviolet to infrared. Between these, and occupying only a small fraction of the entire electromagnetic spectrum, is visible light. This is made up of all the colours of the spectrum, which combine to make white sunlight.

◄ INVISIBLE RAYS
Although we cannot see ultraviolet or infrared rays, we can feel them. Ultraviolet causes sunburn, and life on land is possible only because a lot of ultraviolet is absorbed in the stratosphere. This warms up the stratosphere at high altitude, creating the temperature inversion that puts a cap on the world's weather (see page 13). We feel infrared as heat, and when radiated from the Earth's surface it drives the air currents that cause weather.

WHITE HEAT

Hot objects radiate energy, and the hotter they are, the shorter the wavelength of the radiation they emit. Hot steel radiates long-wave infrared radiation. If it starts glowing red, which has a shorter wavelength, you know it is hotter. If it radiates every colour of the spectrum at once, so it glows white, it is hot enough to melt. Since the Sun radiates energy at even shorter wavelengths, it is hotter still.

NORTHERN LIGHTS ►

Some of the energy given out by the Sun takes the form of a "solar wind" of charged atomic particles. Drawn towards the poles by Earth's magnetic field, they energize air molecules in the upper atmosphere. This creates shimmering curtains of coloured light, called auroras. This is the aurora borealis, or northern lights, glowing in the night sky above Arctic Canada.

Spectrum of colours *is revealed as white light is split*

Light bends *when it passes through the glass*

Beam of white light *shines into a glass prism*

Visible light *is white*

◄ LIGHT AND COLOUR

The white sunlight that lights up the Earth is actually a mixture of all the colours of the spectrum, from short-wave violet to long-wave red. If white light passes through a light-bending glass prism, different wavelengths are bent to different degrees, splitting them into separate colours again. When sunlight interacts with air or water, similar effects create blue skies, red sunsets, and rainbows.

Huge flares of hot gas *erupt from the Sun during active periods*

This flare *is 100 times the size of Earth*

Vast loop of hot gas *is shaped by magnetic forces*

Solar flare *glows orange in this X-ray image*

ENERGY FLUCTUATIONS ►

The amount of energy radiated by the Sun is always changing. It has increased by about 25 per cent since the Earth was formed. It also varies by 0.2 per cent over an 11-year cycle of fluctuating solar activity, and by 0.3 per cent every 85 years. This X-ray image shows a huge solar flare erupting from the Sun's glowing surface during an active period.

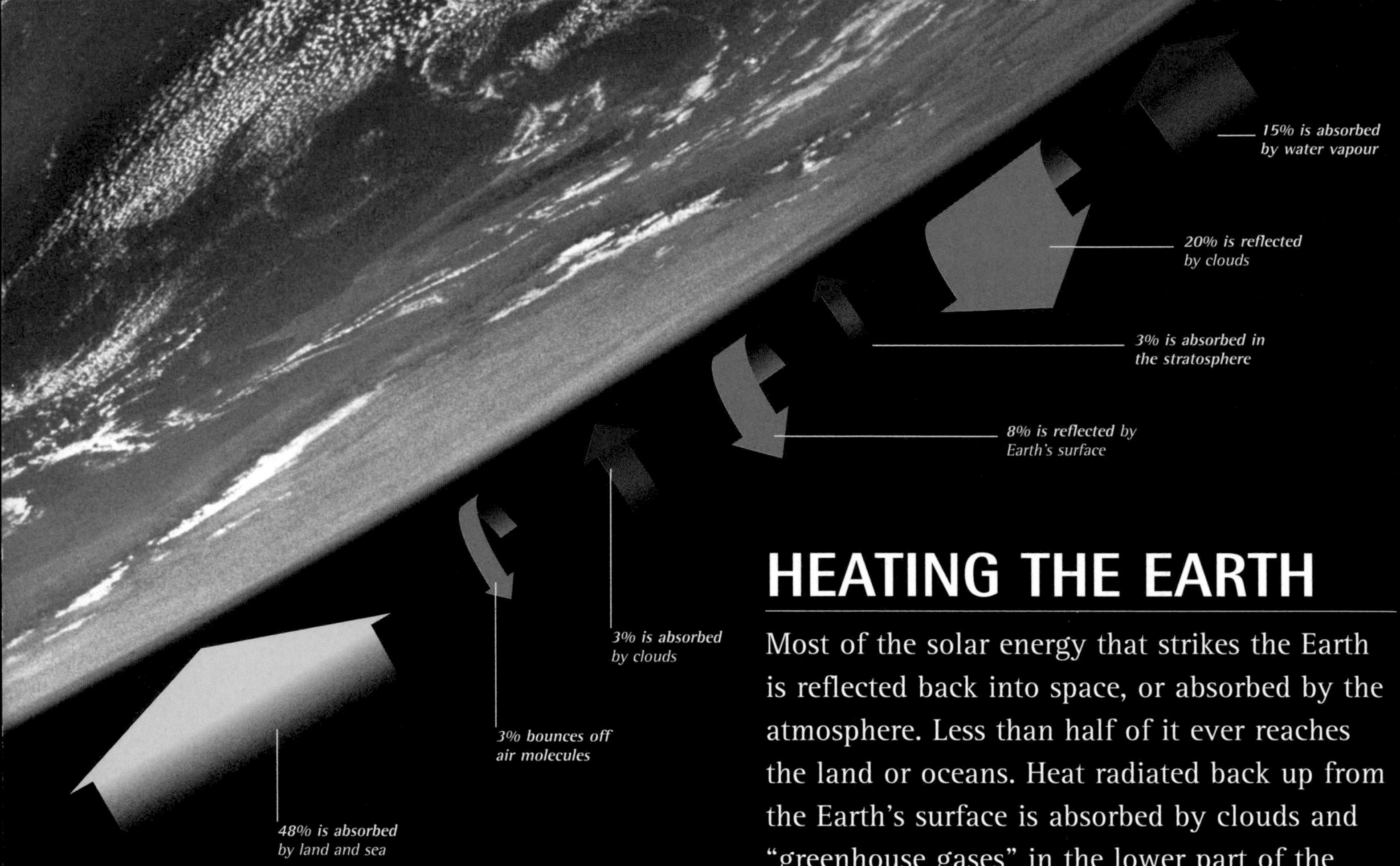

15% is absorbed by water vapour

20% is reflected by clouds

3% is absorbed in the stratosphere

8% is reflected by Earth's surface

3% is absorbed by clouds

3% bounces off air molecules

48% is absorbed by land and sea

HEATING THE EARTH

Most of the solar energy that strikes the Earth is reflected back into space, or absorbed by the atmosphere. Less than half of it ever reaches the land or oceans. Heat radiated back up from the Earth's surface is absorbed by clouds and "greenhouse gases" in the lower part of the atmosphere – the troposphere – which stops some of the heat escaping into space. This means that the troposphere is heated from the bottom, creating thermal air currents that eventually become weather systems.

▲ LOST ENERGY
When solar radiation strikes Earth's atmosphere, nearly a third of the total energy is immediately returned to space. Most of this is reflected by clouds, but some bounces back from air molecules. Some is also reflected by the Earth's surface, especially in icy regions. More energy is absorbed by gases in the stratosphere, and by clouds and water vapour in the troposphere. Just 48 per cent of the incoming solar energy reaches the surface to heat the world's continents and oceans.

KEY

- Energy reflected back into space, with no heating effect
- Energy absorbed in the atmosphere, causing heating
- Energy absorbed by Earth's surface, causing heating

OZONE IN THE STRATOSPHERE

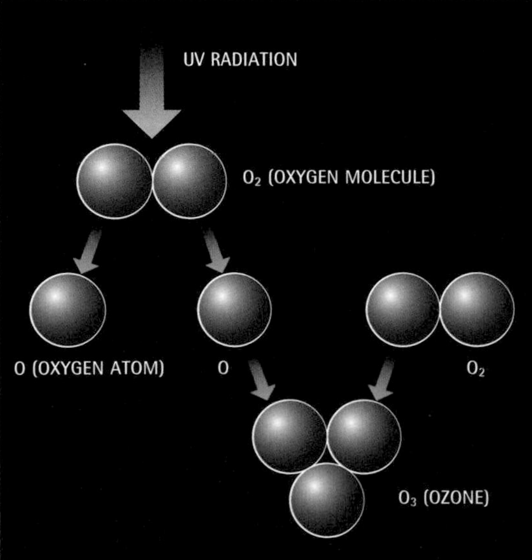

About 3 per cent of the total incoming solar radiation is soaked up by gases in the stratosphere. Much of this is ultraviolet radiation, which is absorbed by oxygen molecules. Each oxygen molecule is made up of two oxygen atoms, so its chemical formula is O_2. The ultraviolet radiation energizes the molecules, and the injection of energy makes some of them split into single oxygen atoms. These then tend to attach to other oxygen molecules, to form a three-atom molecule, called ozone (O_3). But ozone also absorbs ultraviolet radiation (at a different wavelength) and is then split apart in the same way, to make more oxygen. Under natural conditions ozone is created and destroyed at the same rate, soaking up ultraviolet radiation all the time, so its concentration stays constant.

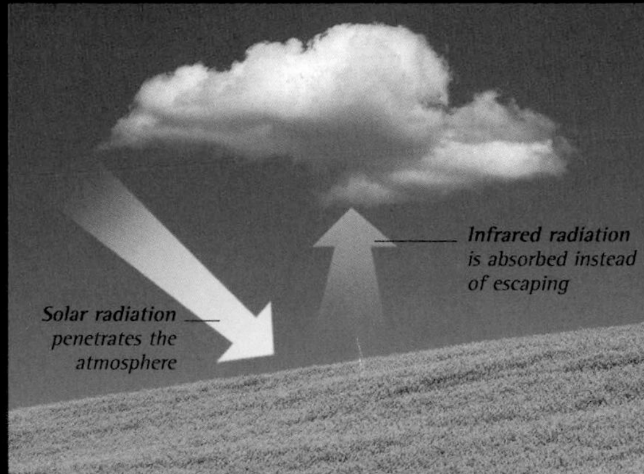

▲ THE GREENHOUSE EFFECT
A lot of solar energy is relatively short-wave radiation that passes straight through the atmosphere to heat the Earth. The heated Earth also radiates energy, but at longer, infrared wavelengths. This radiation is absorbed by "greenhouse gases" in the atmosphere, such as carbon dioxide and water vapour. This warms the atmosphere and keeps the average temperature on Earth roughly 30°C (54°F) higher than on the airless Moon.

A SOLAR FURNACE ►

The Sun's rays can be focused to generate very high temperatures. This works on a small scale using a magnifying glass, but it can also be done on a large scale using mirrors. A solar furnace, such as this one in California, uses a vast array of mirrors to focus solar energy on a single point, and can achieve temperatures of more than 2,000°C (3,600°F).

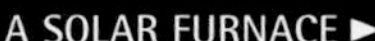

Tower supports the target to be heated.

Mirrors reflect solar rays on to the target

THE ALBEDO EFFECT

Some surfaces reflect more solar energy than others. This reflectivity is called their albedo. The higher the albedo, the less heat energy is absorbed. Ice and snow have an albedo of over 80 per cent, so they act like mirrors, forcing polar explorers to wear anti-glare goggles. Since so little heat is absorbed by the ice, it takes a lot of solar energy to melt it. But if it does melt, it reveals bare rock with an albedo of less than 20 per cent. This absorbs more energy, warms up easily and prevents the formation of more ice.

Weak heating here allows polar ice sheets to form

In the far north energy from the Sun is dispersed

Strong heating effect here creates tropical rainfall

In the tropics energy from the Sun is concentrated

◄ DISPERSED ENERGY

In the tropics, the Sun's rays strike the Earth's surface directly and the Sun's energy is very concentrated. But near the poles, the Sun's rays strike the surface at an angle and the energy is dispersed. So the amount of energy that is absorbed by an area at the Equator is spread over roughly twice that area at the latitude of Oslo. This is why Oslo is so much colder than Nairobi. The difference in the degree of solar heating at various latitudes is the main reason why air masses are set in motion, generating the world's weather systems.

e ⏭ solar energy

Volcanoes spew gases into the atmosphere of Venus

Greenhouse gases make the surface of Venus so hot that it glows

▼ A GREENHOUSE PLANET

Venus is too close to the Sun for oceans to form and soak up carbon dioxide from the atmosphere, as they do on Earth. So all the carbon dioxide produced by its volcanoes has stayed in its atmosphere. This has created an intense greenhouse effect, raising the average surface temperature from an estimated 87°C (190°F) to above 500°C (930°F).

THE SEASONS

As the Earth orbits the Sun, it spins on an axis that is tilted at approximately 23.5 degrees to the vertical. It is always tilted the same way, so in June the North Pole is turned towards the Sun, and in December it is turned away from the Sun. This means that in June the northern hemisphere is heated more intensely than the southern hemisphere, so it is summer in the north and winter in the south. Six months later the situation is reversed, so it is summer in the south and winter in the north.

seasons

21 MARCH

Days are the same length in both north and south

21 JUNE

North Pole

The Arctic enjoys 24-hour summer daylight

The north tilts towards the Sun so is warmer than the south

The south has shorter days than the north

South Pole

THE ORBITING EARTH ► On 21 June, the area within the Arctic Circle is in constant daylight, and because the northern latitudes face the Sun more directly than the southern ones, they enjoy a warm summer. In December, the south is tilted towards the Sun so summer occurs in the southern latitudes. The north is now leaning away from the Sun, which results in the lower temperatures of winter, and constant darkness in the Arctic.

POLAR SEASONS

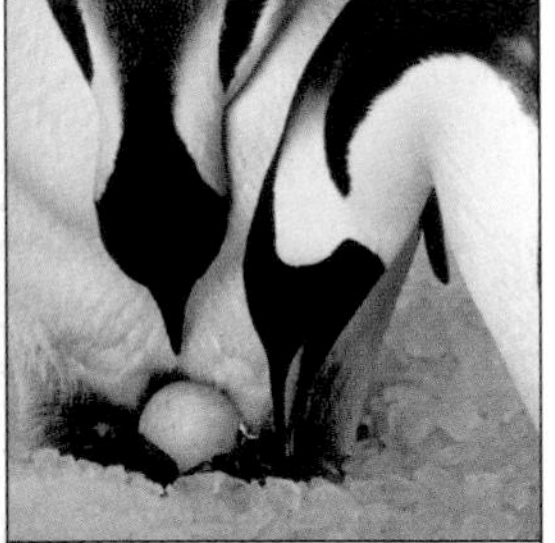

ANTARCTIC WINTER
In winter, the polar regions get very little sunlight, and air temperatures plummet way below freezing. Emperor penguins incubating their eggs on the outskirts of Antarctica have to huddle together to stay warm, and they support the eggs on their feet to stop them freezing solid.

ARCTIC SUMMER
In the summer months, the polar regions experience almost continuous daylight. On the Arctic tundra this causes a burst of life, as plants flower, insects breed, and migrant birds, like this eider duck, arrive in their millions to lay eggs and rear their young on the brief abundance of food.

▲ WINTER
In both the north and south mid-latitudes the winters are cold, with short days and long nights. Some trees survive by losing their leaves and lying dormant, and many animals either sleep through the winter or migrate to warmer regions.

▲ SPRING
Spring brings rising temperatures and longer days. Many low-growing plants burst into flower on the sunlit ground beneath the leafless trees. Animals emerge from their winter refuges or return from migration and start to breed.

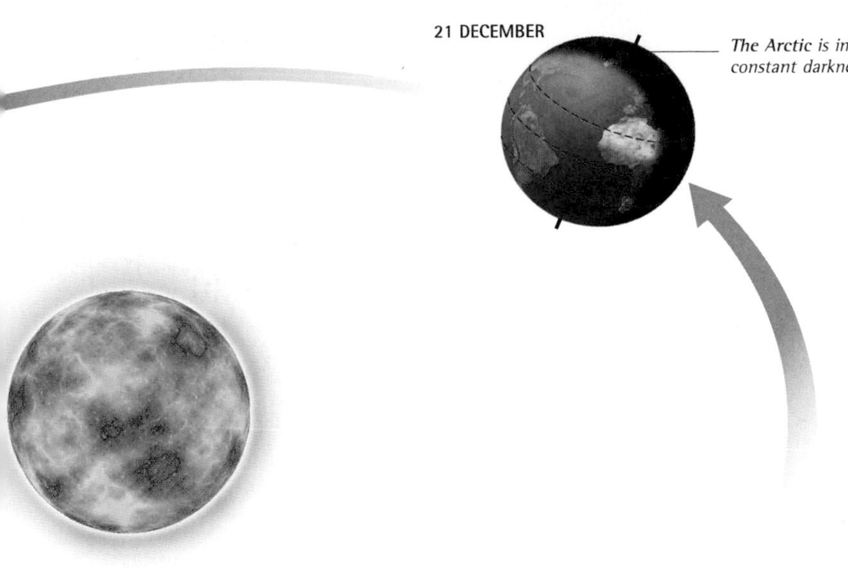

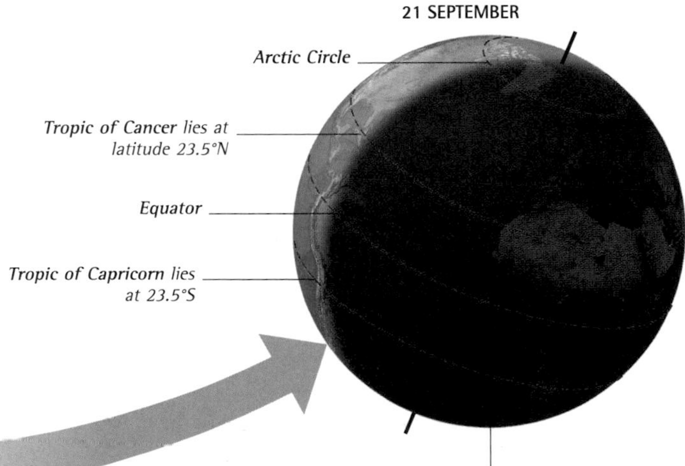

▲ SNOW IN THE TROPICS
The higher you go, the lower the air temperature gets. So mountains are always colder than the surrounding lowlands. Even in the tropics, high peaks, such as Kilimanjaro in Africa, are capped with snow. The route up to the summit passes through a succession of climatic zones that correspond to those of the different latitudes from the Equator to the poles.

TROPICAL SEASONS

WET SEASON
In the tropics, the zone of maximum sunlight intensity shifts north and south over the year. This draws the tropical storm systems north and south, creating wet and dry seasons. In the wet season, the savannahs of East Africa experience torrential rain falling from huge thunderclouds that build up over the grasslands.

DRY SEASON
In June, the thunderstorm belt retreats to the north of the East African savannahs, and the rain stops falling. The dry season lasts until November, and by then the soil has turned to dust. The grass withers and burns, but tough trees like acacias survive by tapping into water from deep underground with their long roots.

▲ SUMMER
In summer, the days are long and hot. In coastal regions there is enough rain for plants to keep growing and produce lush foliage. But in the middle of continents droughts limit tree growth, resulting in extensive prairie grasslands.

▲ AUTUMN
As the autumn days get shorter, temperatures drop and rainfall often increases. In regions with icy winters, trees prepare to lose their foliage. They stop producing green chlorophyll, so the leaves turn shades of brown, yellow, and red.

WARM AND COLD AIR

The power that drives our weather is heat from the Sun. But the Sun does not heat the Earth's surface evenly – areas near the Equator receive much more heat than areas near the poles. This means that the air in the lower part of the atmosphere is warmed to different degrees at different latitudes. Because warm air usually rises through cooler air, these differences in temperature set the air moving. This creates systems of circulating air that redistribute heat around the globe.

Hot air inside the balloon makes it rise through the cooler air around it

***Air must be heated** by the burner to keep the balloon rising*

▲ RISING WARM AIR
As warmed air expands, it take up more space. This means that its original volume contains fewer air molecules, so it is not as dense. Since warm air is less dense than the same volume of cooler air, it weighs less, and tends to float up through cooler, heavier air. It is this effect that carries a hot-air balloon up into the sky. But as the air expands, it starts to cool – and when its temperature is the same as the surrounding air, it stops rising.

EXPANDING AIR

Cold air molecules | Warm air molecules

Air molecules are held together by forces of attraction. But they are constantly moving, and this works against the forces of attraction. The amount that the molecules move is related to their energy. Cold air contains little energy, so the forces of attraction draw the molecules in cold air close together. Heating the air gives the molecules more energy, making them move about more and move apart. So the same number of air molecules take up more space if they are heated. This is why air expands when it is warmed up.

▲ RISING THERMALS
If air is heated unevenly from below, part of the air mass becomes warmer and less dense than the air around it. This warm, light air moves upwards, and cooler, heavier air flows in at low level to replace it. On a tropical island, for example, the midday Sun makes the land warmer than the surrounding ocean. The hot ground warms the air above the island, so it rises. Cooler air then flows in from the ocean, replacing the air that has risen, and is warmed up in turn.

▲ HIGH-LEVEL COOLING
As warm air rises it keeps expanding, because at high altitude there is less atmospheric pressure to squash it together. This type of expansion uses energy, and makes the air cool down. Eventually the air stops expanding and rising, and spreads out sideways instead. The same happens if rising air reaches a zone where the surrounding air has the same density as it does. This is why cumulonimbus clouds spread out sideways when they reach the base of the stratosphere.

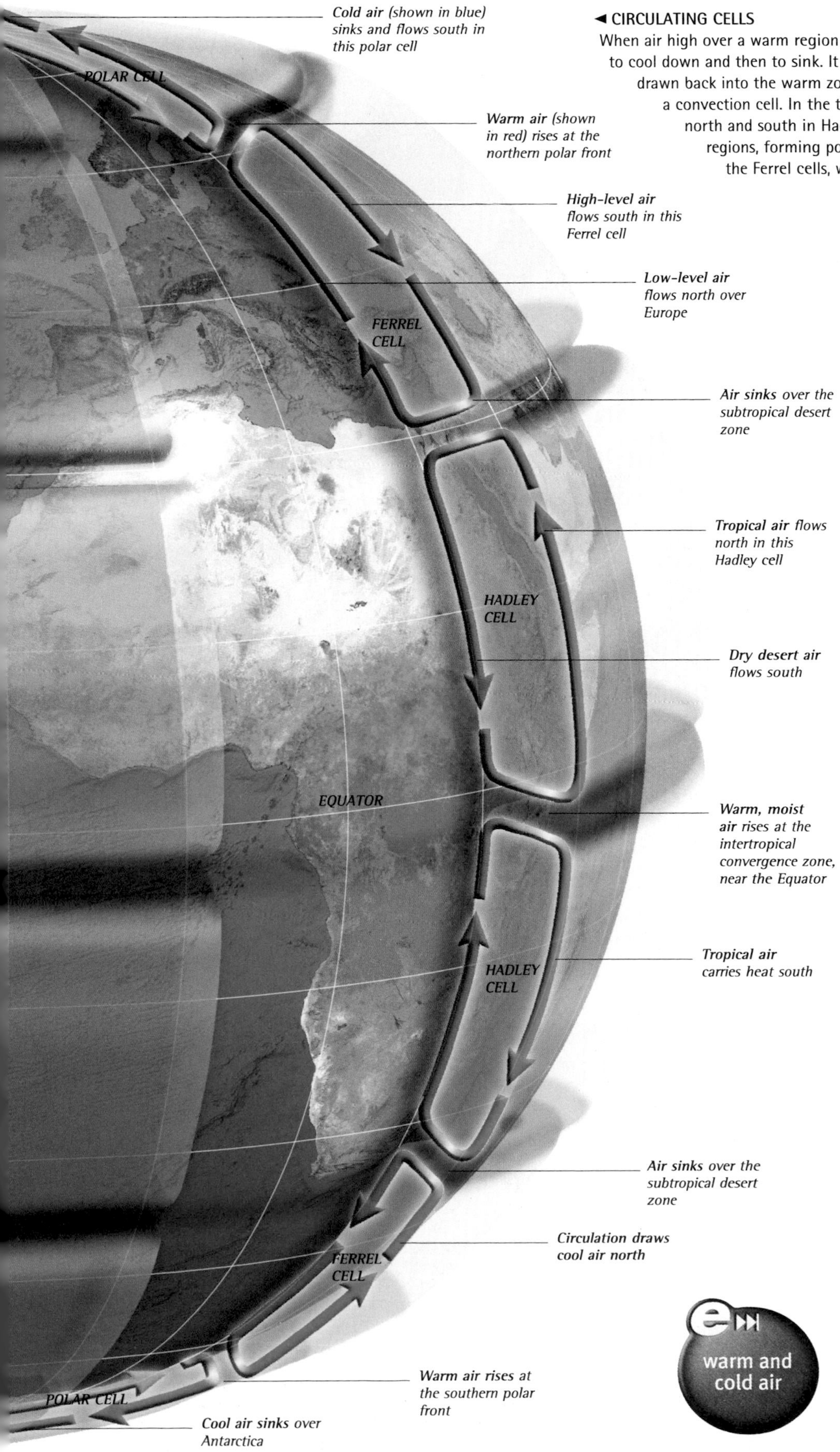

Cold air (shown in blue) sinks and flows south in this polar cell

POLAR CELL

Warm air (shown in red) rises at the northern polar front

High-level air flows south in this Ferrel cell

Low-level air flows north over Europe

FERREL CELL

Air sinks over the subtropical desert zone

Tropical air flows north in this Hadley cell

HADLEY CELL

Dry desert air flows south

EQUATOR

Warm, moist air rises at the intertropical convergence zone, near the Equator

Tropical air carries heat south

HADLEY CELL

Air sinks over the subtropical desert zone

Circulation draws cool air north

FERREL CELL

Warm air rises at the southern polar front

POLAR CELL

Cool air sinks over Antarctica

◄ CIRCULATING CELLS

When air high over a warm region is pushed aside by more rising warm air, it starts to cool down and then to sink. It returns almost to ground level, and may be drawn back into the warm zone to replace the rising warm air. This is called a convection cell. In the tropics, warm air rising near the Equator flows north and south in Hadley cells. A similar circulation occurs in the polar regions, forming polar cells. Between the Hadley and polar cells are the Ferrel cells, which circulate in the opposite direction.

▲ RAINFOREST ZONE

Where warm air is rising, it creates a zone of low atmospheric pressure. The zone of rising warm air near the Equator where the Hadley cells come together is known as the intertropical convergence zone, or ITCZ. Here, the rising warm air contains moisture that forms clouds and tropical rain, leading to the growth of rainforests.

▲ DESERT ZONE

Where air is sinking, there is a greater weight of air, creating a zone of high atmospheric pressure. Sinking air stops clouds forming, so it hardly ever rains. This leads to the formation of deserts, such as the Sahara and the Kalahari, in the subtropical high-pressure zones. It also creates polar deserts, such the Dry Valleys of Antarctica, pictured here.

▲ MIXING ZONE

The zone of rising air at the boundary between a polar cell and a Ferrel cell is called the polar front. Here, cool polar air pushes beneath warmer air moving from the subtropical zones, forcing it upwards. In the process, the warm and cold air masses mix in complex ways. This creates circulating weather systems that cause the changeable climate of regions such as northern Europe, above.

warm and cold air

THE CORIOLIS EFFECT

The Earth's atmosphere is constantly moving, as warm air flows from the tropics towards the poles, and cold air flows back from the poles towards the Equator. But this circulation pattern is affected by another movement – our planet is always rotating on its axis. The Earth's spin has the effect of deflecting the north-south airflow towards the east and west. This deflection, known as the Coriolis effect, is strongest near the poles, but non-existent at the Equator.

NEWTON'S FIRST LAW

In 1687, the British scientist Isaac Newton (1642–1727) published his three laws of motion. The first of these laws states that a moving object will maintain its speed and direction, unless it is acted on by some other force. This is why air moving over the Earth at a certain speed tends to maintain that speed, even if the Earth is spinning below it at a different rate. As a result, the air swerves away from a straight course over the Earth's surface.

CORIOLIS

Physicist and mathematician Gustave-Gaspard de Coriolis (1792–1843) became assistant professor of mathematics at the Ecole Polytechnique in Paris in 1816. He carried out research in several fields, including hydraulics. His study of waterwheels led to his explanation of the way fluids and objects move across the surface of the spinning Earth. His paper describing this motion – now known as the Coriolis effect – was published in 1835. Coriolis died in Paris at the age of 51.

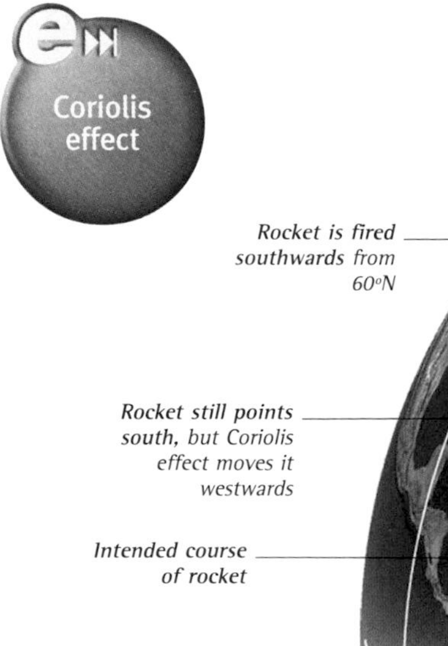

DRIFTING OFF COURSE ▲
One way to picture the Coriolis effect is to imagine a rocket being launched. The rocket base is at latitude 60°N. As the Earth is spinning, the base is actually travelling eastwards at a speed of 835 kph (519 mph). The rocket is launched towards the Equator. But as it heads south, it also maintains its eastwards speed, according to Newton's first law. But the Earth beneath it is moving east at a faster rate. The rocket lags behind, so it actually drifts west relative to the Earth's surface. Now imagine that a rocket is being launched from a base near the Equator. The opposite happens. The rocket starts from a place that is travelling east at 1,670 kph (1,038 mph). As it shoots north, the rocket maintains this eastward speed. But the ground below is moving east more slowly, so the rocket drifts east relative to the Earth's surface.

VIEW OF THE NORTHERN HEMISPHERE

EQUATOR

NORTH POLE

180°

90°E

60°N

90°W

The ground at the Equator is moving at 1,670 kph (1,038 mph)

At 60°N, the ground is moving at 835 kph (519 mph)

EQUATOR

SOUTH POLE

0°

180°

60°S

30°S

90°W

VIEW OF THE SOUTHERN HEMISPHERE

◄ THE SPINNING EARTH
The Earth is spinning, so anything on its surface is moving round with it. But the speed at which any place on Earth moves depends on where it is. At the Equator, the ground travels right round the Earth's circumference each day and hurtles eastwards at 1,670 kph (1,038 mph). But near the poles, the ground travels a shorter distance, so it moves more slowly.

MOVING AIR ►

Air currents are influenced by the Coriolis effect in a similar way to rockets. In the northern hemisphere, the Coriolis effect makes moving air tend to swerve to the right of its original direction, relative to the rotating surface of the Earth. Air moving north turns east, while air moving south turns west. In the southern hemisphere the situation is reversed, and moving air tends to swerve to the left of its original direction. This explains why large air masses don't move directly from the Equator to the poles or back again. The Coriolis effect therefore has a big influence on the direction of wind and weather systems as they move around the world.

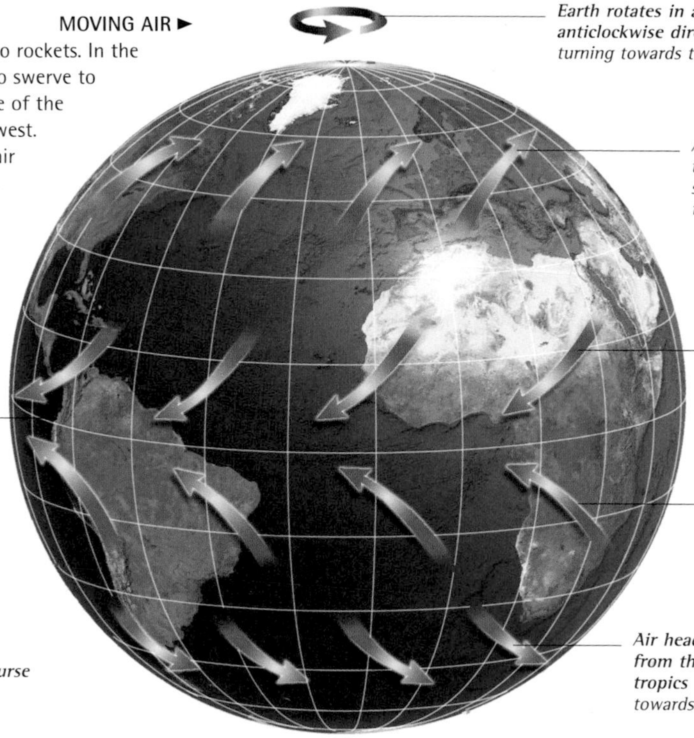

Earth rotates in an anticlockwise direction, *turning towards the east*

Air moving away from the northern tropics *swerves right, towards the east*

Equator

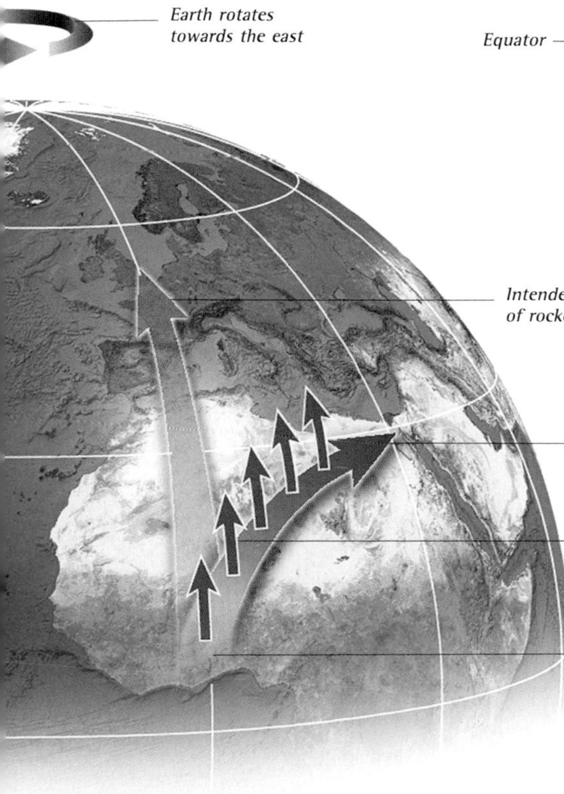

Northern air moving towards the Equator *swerves right, towards the west*

Southern air moving towards the Equator *turns left, but also towards the west*

Air heading away from the southern tropics *turns left, towards the east*

Earth rotates towards the east

Intended course of rocket

Coriolis effect *moves the rocket eastwards*

Rocket still points north, *but slips off course*

Rocket is fired northwards *from near the Equator*

◄ DOWN THE DRAIN

Water draining down a plughole is often said to swirl in different directions north and south of the Equator. In fact, the Coriolis effect is virtually undetectable on a small scale, such as in a sink or bath. So the water may swirl in either direction, usually because it was moving that way already.

THE CORIOLIS EFFECT AND THE WEATHER

SPINNING STORMS

Tropical revolving storms, such as hurricanes, need the Coriolis effect to help them to start spinning. These storms are fuelled by warm water in tropical oceans, but they never build up near the Equator, because there is no Coriolis effect there to start them rotating.

MARITIME CLIMATE

In the northern mid-latitudes, the Coriolis effect makes moving air turn towards the east. This sweeps mild, wet air off the North Atlantic and over north-western Europe, helping to make the climate there wetter and milder than in eastern Canada, on the other side of the ocean.

OCEAN WINDS

The islands on the far eastern edge of the Caribbean are known as the Windward Islands, because they lie in the path of the trade winds that blow off the North Atlantic. These steady winds are the result of tropical air being deflected westwards by the Coriolis effect.

PREVAILING WINDS

In many places in the world, the wind normally blows from one direction. In western Europe, for example, the wind usually comes from the southwest. This is known as the prevailing wind. Prevailing winds blow most reliably over the open ocean, far from land. Large landmasses tend to disrupt prevailing winds because they heat up and cool down faster than the oceans. This creates local, seasonal winds which can vary the direction of the prevailing wind.

Earth spins in an anticlockwise direction

Westwards swerve creates north-east trade wind

SUBTROPICAL ZONE

EQUATOR

INTERTROPICAL CONVERGENCE ZONE

Warm air rises at the intertropical convergence zone

Cooler air sinks in the subtropics

SUBTROPI

Westwards swerve creates south-east trade wind

High-level winds swerve towards the east

Low-level winds swerve towards the west

SPIRALLING AIR ►
Prevailing winds are caused by the effect of the Earth's rotation – the Coriolis effect – on cells of circulating air. For example, in the tropics, air circulates by rising up and away from the Equator, then sinks and heads back towards the Equator at low level. But the Coriolis effect makes this circulating air swerve off course. The high-level air swerves towards the east, and the low-level air swerves to the west, forming a spiral of circulating air. This creates low-level winds that blow from the north-east in the northern tropics, and from the south-east in the southern tropics. There are similar air circulation patterns over the mid-latitudes and the polar regions.

▲ TRADE WINDS
In the tropics, the prevailing winds are known as the trade winds, because they were vital to trading ships in the days of sail. The northeast trade wind was used by ships sailing westwards across the Atlantic to the Caribbean – a route that has been followed by sailors since it was discovered by Christopher Columbus. A similar southeast trade wind blows across the Pacific.

▲ CALM ZONES
Near the Equator, at the intertropical convergence zone, there is little wind. The trade winds converge here and the airflow is mainly upwards. At sea, this calm zone is known as the doldrums. Calm zones also occur in the subtropics, when air is sinking. They include the weed-strewn Sargasso Sea in the North Atlantic – a place where sailing ships could be stuck for weeks.

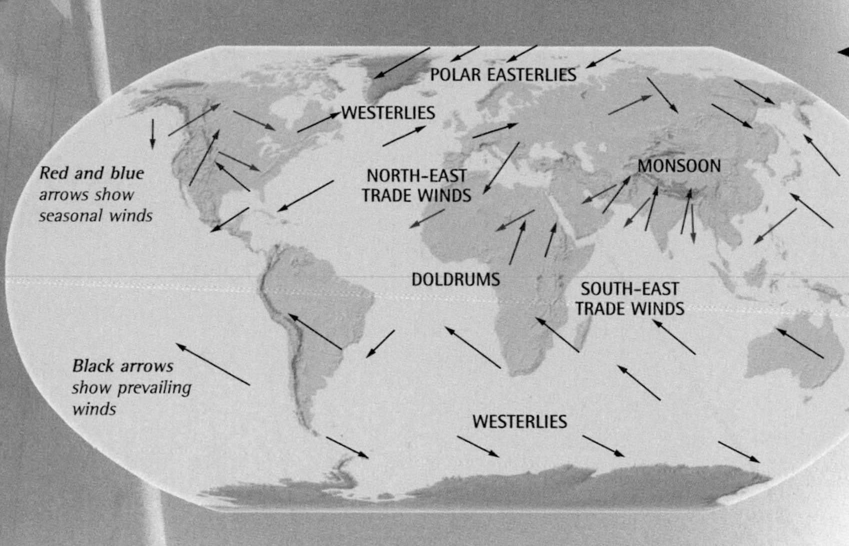

◄ GLOBAL WINDS

Moving outwards from the Equator towards the poles, the general pattern of prevailing winds is tropical trade winds, then mid-latitude westerlies, then polar easterlies. This pattern is clearest in the southern hemisphere, where there are large areas of open ocean. In the north, the vast continents of Asia, northern Africa, and North America create seasonal winds, such as the south Asian monsoon, which confuse the normal pattern of winds.

e ▸▸ prevailing winds

WESTERLIES ►

In the mid-latitudes, prevailing winds over the oceans are called westerlies because they blow from a westerly direction. In the north Atlantic, these westerlies carry salty maritime air over Ireland. This keeps the Irish climate mild and damp, but trees are sometimes bent over by the constant west wind. In the same way, prevailing westerlies dominate the climate of New Zealand, which lies in the southern mid-latitude zone.

High winds loaded with salt spray make visibility poor

Ships plunge through mountainous waves

POLAR EASTERLIES ►

In the polar regions, the prevailing winds blow from the east and are known as the polar easterlies. These winds drive floating pack ice westwards around the coasts of Antarctica, and push ice clockwise around the Arctic Ocean. Not all the polar easterlies blow reliably all year round, and these winds were of little use to sailors because the polar oceans are mostly frozen at the surface.

◄ THE ROARING FORTIES

The further you travel from the Equator, the more the average wind speed increases. This is very apparent in the southern ocean that surrounds Antarctica. At 40°S, the prevailing westerlies are powerful enough to be known as the "Roaring Forties". The wind speeds increase the further south you go, creating the "Furious Fifties" and "Shrieking Sixties". These winds partly account for the deadly reputation of Cape Horn at the tip of South America, which lies at about 56°S. The seas there are so stormy that shipwrecks used to be common.

OCEANS AND CONTINENTS

The main cause of the world's weather is air circulating from the tropics to the polar regions and back. This circulating air is pushed off-course by the Coriolis effect. But this pattern is modified by the continents, which warm up and cool down more rapidly than the oceans. This creates temperature differences between land and sea that make air circulate in other directions. Slowly-changing ocean temperatures also make coastal climates less extreme than continental climates.

oceans and continents

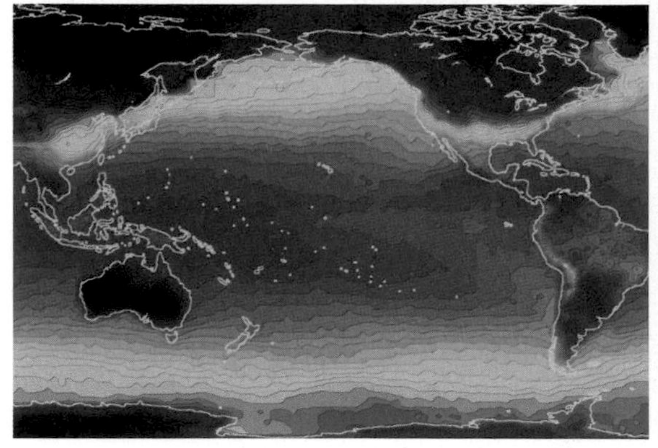

▲ LAND AND SEA TEMPERATURES
The sea warms and cools more slowly than the land. Scientists call this thermal inertia. It means that oceans never get as hot or cold as continents at the same latitude. This satellite image of temperatures in January shows North America and northern Asia as very cold (deep blue), and Australia as very hot (deep red), but the differences in ocean temperatures are much less extreme.

▲ ISLAND PARADISE
Islands and coasts always have much milder climates than nearby continents, because the ocean stops them getting too hot or too cold. The island of Tenerife, off North Africa, has a warm and pleasant climate, even though it lies on the same latitude as the Sahara Desert – one of the hottest places on Earth.

COOL WATER ►
The thermal inertia of oceans ensures that they never get very hot or very cold. This is why the sea feels cool in summer after you've been sitting on a hot beach. In winter in the polar regions, the sea is warmer than the frozen land. The water may be close to freezing, but the thick ice sheets of Greenland and Antarctica are much colder.

Icebergs are huge chunks of ice that have broken off the polar ice caps

▼ ICY CURRENTS
Ocean currents move heat around the globe, just like air currents do. Warm ocean currents flowing away from the tropics carry heat to the polar regions, and cold currents flowing from the poles help to cool the tropics. The cold currents may even carry icebergs into warmer waters. It was an iceberg like this, drifting south from Greenland, that sank the *Titanic* in 1912.

◄ HIGH AND LOW PRESSURE
In winter, air above the continents cools more than air above oceans. This cool air sinks, creating high air pressure. This prevents cloud formation and rainfall, as in the cold Gobi Desert in the heart of Asia. In summer the opposite happens – rising air over continents creates low pressure. These seasonal changes affect the air circulation over a wide area.

CONTINENTAL CLIMATE

FREEZING WINTERS
Coastal regions have mild winters and cool summers, but temperatures in the middle of continents are much more extreme. At Verkhoyansk in Siberia, the winter temperature can drop to –68°C (–90°F), making it the coldest town in the northern hemisphere. It is colder than the North Pole, because the pole lies on a relatively thin sheet of ice floating on an ocean. The ocean stops the temperature falling far below freezing.

HOT SUMMERS
Verkhoyansk (shown here) lies too far north to get very warm in summer. But the summer temperature rises high enough to melt all the snow and ice and enable people to grow crops in the thawed-out surface soil. Further south, in central Siberia, the temperature can rise to 30°C (86°F), even though it may have fallen to –30°C (–22°F) in the winter. Big temperature changes like this are typical of continental climates.

THE OCEAN CONVEYOR

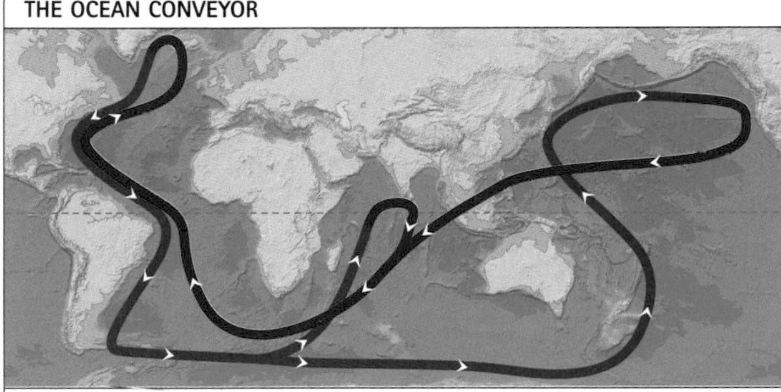

The ocean currents are linked together in a system that carries water all round the globe, redistributing heat around the world. It is like a giant conveyor belt of moving water, looping through the world's oceans, so it is sometimes known as the ocean conveyor. Scientists call this the thermohaline circulation, because it is driven by the temperature (*thermo* means "heat") and saltiness (*haline* means "salty") of the water. Low temperatures and high salt content make ocean water dense and heavy, so it sinks. In the North Atlantic, cold, salty water sinking near Greenland is one of the main "engines" driving the conveyor. As this water sinks and flows south, it is replaced by warm water flowing north in the North Atlantic Drift, an extension of the Gulf Stream.

▼ THE GULF STREAM
The Gulf Stream carries warm water from the Gulf of Mexico into the North Atlantic. This warm water makes the climate of northern Europe warmer than it would be otherwise. The influence of the Gulf Stream is particularly noticeable in Britain and Ireland, which lie on the same latitude as Labrador in Canada on the other side of the Atlantic, but have far milder winters. If the Gulf Stream stopped flowing, northern Europe would freeze in winter.

Tropical palm trees grow in the Scilly Isles, off southwest Britain, which lie in the Gulf Stream

AIR MASSES

As air circulates around the Earth, it passes over warm and cold oceans and continents. These alter the characteristics of the air that moves over them. They can make the air warm or cold, dry or moist. The slower the air mass is moving, the longer it will stay over a particular area, such as a warm ocean, and the bigger the influence of the ocean on the air. This creates four main types of air mass, each with different combinations of temperature and water content.

MULTIPLE AIR MASSES

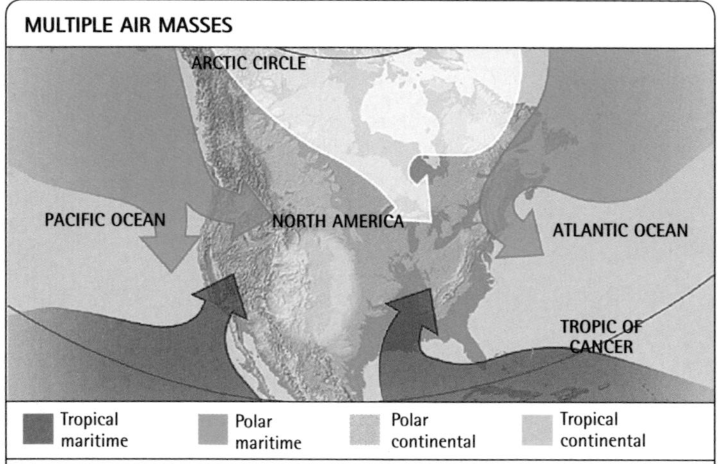

Tropical maritime | Polar maritime | Polar continental | Tropical continental

The weather at any place on Earth is usually influenced by two or more air masses of different types. In North America, for example, the weather is influenced by six air masses. Cool polar continental air moves south from Arctic Canada, while polar maritime air flows in from the northern oceans. Warm, moist tropical maritime air can move in from tropical oceans, while tropical continental air develops over the southern core of the continent.

▲ SEASONAL SHIFTS
Ocean temperatures do not change very much over the year, but in the middle of a continent, winter and summer temperatures can vary by as much as 60°C (108°F). This alters the nature of continental air masses, and the way they interact with more stable maritime air masses. In spring, continental air moving south from Canada over the USA is much colder and drier than the maritime air moving north from the Gulf of Mexico and their interaction causes spring tornadoes.

◄ TROPICAL CONTINENTAL
When air moves slowly over a hot, dry continent, it can gain a lot of heat and develop into a hot, dry tropical continental air mass. This type of air causes the dry seasons in regions near tropical deserts, such as the Sahel, south of the Sahara in Africa. Here, hot, dry air is drawn south off the desert by rising air near the Equator. If it keeps moving south, it can cause droughts.

◄ POLAR CONTINENTAL
Air that passes over cold, dry continental regions, such as Canada and Siberia, is both cooled and dried, so it becomes a cold, dry polar continental air mass. These regions become extremely cold in winter, with ground temperatures that fall well below freezing, so the air becomes very cold too. If the air mass is then drawn over a warmer region, it can make temperatures there plummet, but since it contains little moisture it produces dry weather with clear blue skies.

◄ TROPICAL MARITIME
Air that passes over warm oceans picks up warmth and moisture, creating a tropical maritime air mass. Warm air can hold more water vapour than cold air, so these air masses are very wet and often bring heavy rain. During the Indian monsoon, for example, a tropical maritime air mass moving north from the Indian Ocean pours virtually non-stop torrential rain on the subcontinent for two or three months, and often causes serious flooding.

◄ POLAR MARITIME
Air moving over cold oceans is cooled by contact with the water, but does not become as cold as air that passes over cold continents. It also picks up moisture, but cool air cannot hold as much water vapour as warm air. The result is a cool, moist polar maritime air mass. In Tasmania, Australia, the cool, moist maritime air moving in from the ocean has encouraged the growth of temperate rainforests, which flourish in the rainy, but frost-free, climate.

CHANGING AIR MASSES

Although maritime air masses carry a lot of moisture, the land they pass over does not always get much rain. This is because the nature of an air mass can change. If it passes over a mountain ridge, for example, moisture in the air will fall as rain over the mountains, and the air mass will change from moist to dry. This creates a "rain shadow" – a region on the other side of the mountains that receives very little rain. This effect is very pronounced in South America. There, maritime air moving west off the Pacific Ocean pours its rain over the high Andes mountains. The land between the Pacific coast and the mountains – Chile – is therefore lush and fertile, but on the other side of the mountains, the rain shadow effect has created a desert in Patagonia.

Fishing ships have to cope with poor visibility, caused by fog over the Benguela Current

▲ A FOG DESERT
Ocean currents can also change the nature of air masses. Where warm, moist air sweeps off the Atlantic on to southwest Africa, it passes over the cold Benguela Current, which flows north from Antarctica. The contact with the cold water turns the water vapour in the air into fog and rain. By the time the air reaches land on the Skeleton Coast of Namibia, it has lost most of its moisture. As a result, the land is a barren desert, although plants and animals can survive there by gathering moisture from the fog that rolls in over the coast.

WEATHER FRONTS

When two air masses meet, they do not simply mix. One is usually colder than the other. Sometimes the colder, heavier air pushes underneath the warmer air. Sometimes the warmer, lighter air slides up over the cooler air. Either way, the warmer air is forced upwards, and this often creates clouds and rain. The place where two air masses meet is called a front. Some fronts are regular features of the atmosphere and can extend for thousands of kilometres. Other fronts are more short-lived and local, but all fronts mark a boundary between air masses.

Cold air descends over the Arctic

POLAR CELL

Warm air is pushed up at the Polar Front

Air flows away from the front at high level

POLAR FRONT

FERREL CELL

Air sinks over the desert zone and warms up

HADLEY CELL

Hot air rises near the Equator

POLAR FRONT ►

Two of the most important large-scale weather fronts are the northern and southern polar fronts. These mark the boundaries between cold polar air and warm tropical air. At the northern polar front, cold, heavy air flowing away from the Arctic pushes beneath warmer air that is flowing from the tropics. The warmer air is forced up along a sloping front, and some flows north, towards the pole.

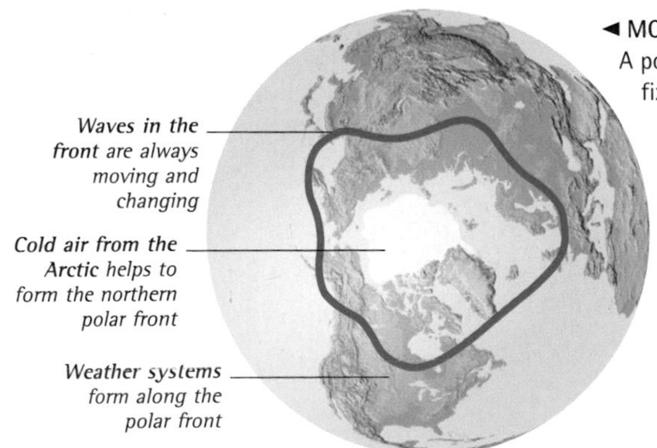

◄ MOVING WAVES

A polar front does not simply encircle the Earth at a fixed latitude. Some air masses push further north or south than others, and this distorts the polar front into an irregular shape with four or five waves in it. These waves move slowly east around the globe with the prevailing winds, and are constantly changing their shape. Waves in the front cause weather systems to form. They are responsible for the changeable weather that affects the regions that lie under the polar fronts (see page 37).

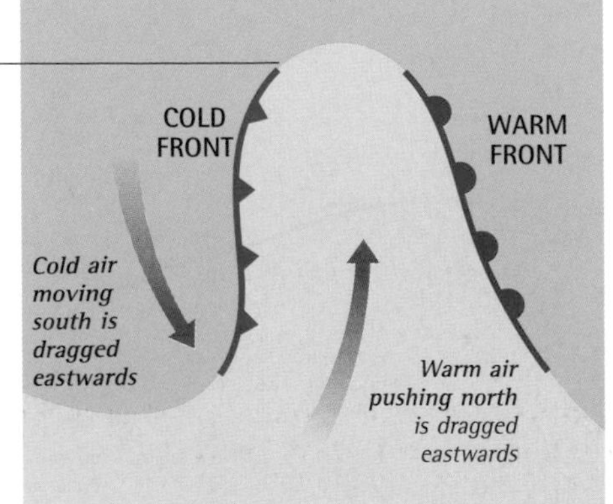

LOCAL FRONTS ►

When the warm and cold air masses on either side of the polar front push north and south, they tend to squeeze past each other to create a wave in the front. At the northern polar front, for example, a mass of warm air may push north while a mass of cold air moves south. Meanwhile, both air masses are also working their way east, and their advancing boundaries form local fronts. The leading edge of the moving warm air mass is marked by a warm front, and the leading edge of the cold air mass forms a cold front.

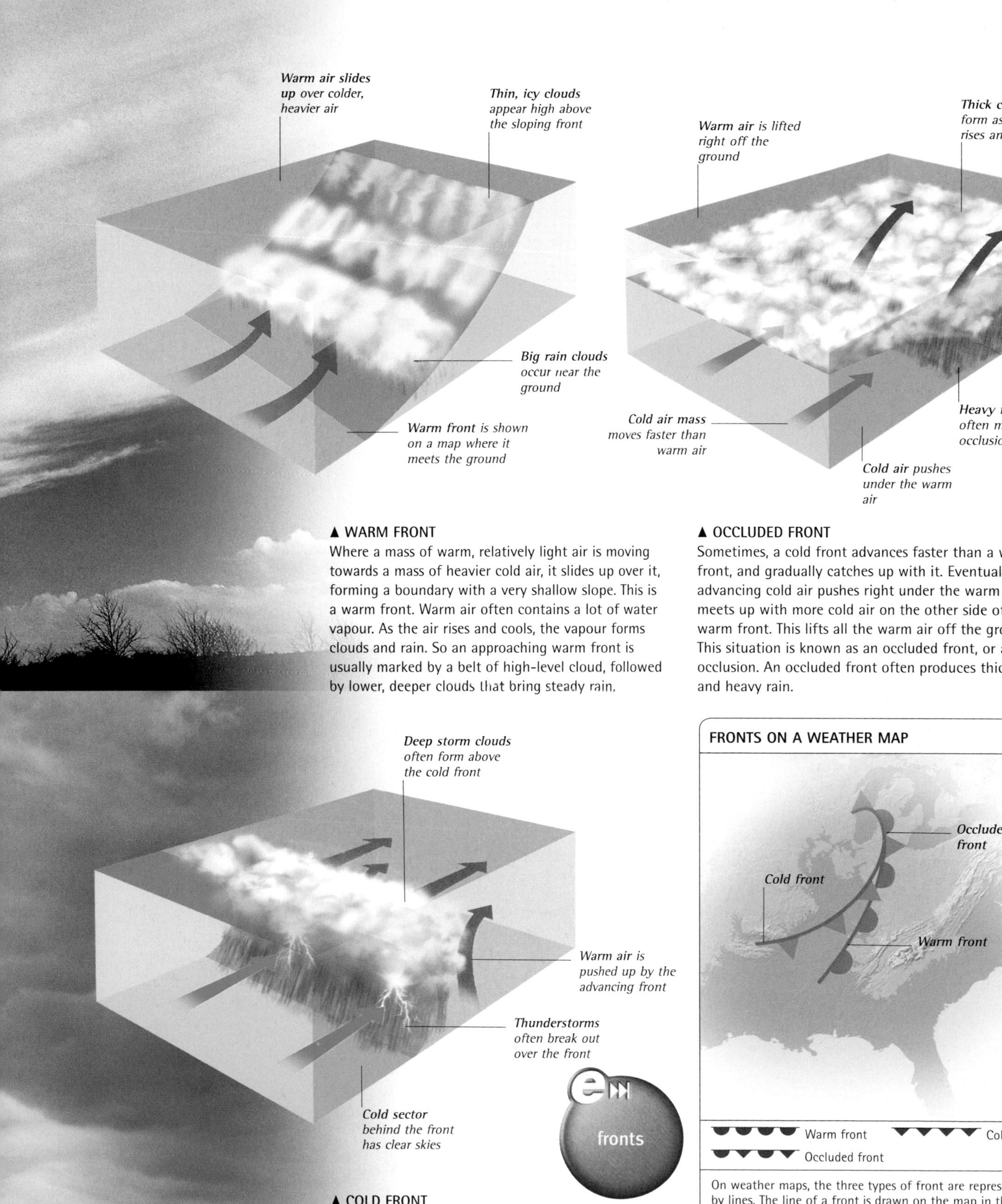

▲ WARM FRONT

Where a mass of warm, relatively light air is moving towards a mass of heavier cold air, it slides up over it, forming a boundary with a very shallow slope. This is a warm front. Warm air often contains a lot of water vapour. As the air rises and cools, the vapour forms clouds and rain. So an approaching warm front is usually marked by a belt of high-level cloud, followed by lower, deeper clouds that bring steady rain.

▲ OCCLUDED FRONT

Sometimes, a cold front advances faster than a warm front, and gradually catches up with it. Eventually, the advancing cold air pushes right under the warm air and meets up with more cold air on the other side of the warm front. This lifts all the warm air off the ground. This situation is known as an occluded front, or an occlusion. An occluded front often produces thick clouds and heavy rain.

▲ COLD FRONT

Where a mass of dense, relatively heavy, cold air is moving towards a mass of lighter warm air, the cold air pushes under the warm air, forming a boundary with a steep slope. This is a cold front. The warm air is pushed up quite fast. If it contains a lot of water vapour, this forms big storm clouds that develop in a narrow band along the front. These cause brief, but often heavy, rain showers, followed by clear blue skies.

FRONTS ON A WEATHER MAP

Warm front — Cold front — Occluded front

On weather maps, the three types of front are represented by lines. The line of a front is drawn on the map in the position where the front boundary touches the ground. The line of a cold front is marked by blue triangles that point in the direction the front is moving. The line of a warm front is marked by red semicircles. An occluded front is indicated by alternate triangles and semicircles. Since an occluded front is caused by a cold front catching up with a warm front, the frontal symbols often come together and merge to mark the occlusion, as shown on this weather map of the southeast USA.

HIGHS AND LOWS

The weather in mid-latitude regions, such as Europe, is dominated by weather systems that move from west to east. They form at the fronts that divide warm and cold air masses. The warmer, lighter air forms a zone of low pressure, where the air tends to rise. The surrounding air swirls into this zone, sucked in by the low pressure. This creates a moving weather system known as a depression, or a low. The high-pressure zones between lows are called anticyclones, or highs.

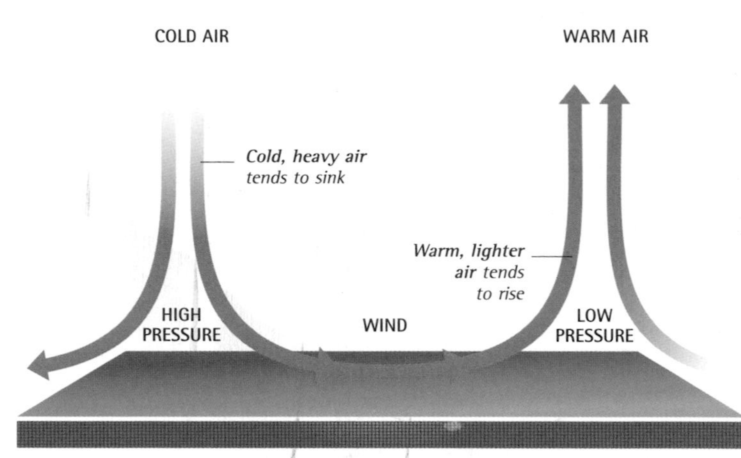

▲ AIR FLOW
Cold air is denser and heavier than warm air, so it tends to sink. This means that the atmospheric pressure beneath a cold air mass is often higher than it is beneath a nearby warm air mass. Surface air is squeezed out of the high-pressure zone, and flows towards the low-pressure zone in the form of wind. When it reaches the centre of the low-pressure zone it is pulled upwards. This allows yet more air to be sucked in at low level.

highs and lows

ANTICYCLONE ►
Air spilling out from a high-pressure zone as wind is influenced by the Coriolis effect (see pages 22–23). This makes it swerve to the right (clockwise) in the northern hemisphere, or to the left (anticlockwise) in the southern hemisphere. The winds in these anticyclones are usually fairly light. Anticyclones themselves often move quite slowly, blocking the movement of other weather systems, such as depressions, and sometimes creating the same weather for weeks on end.

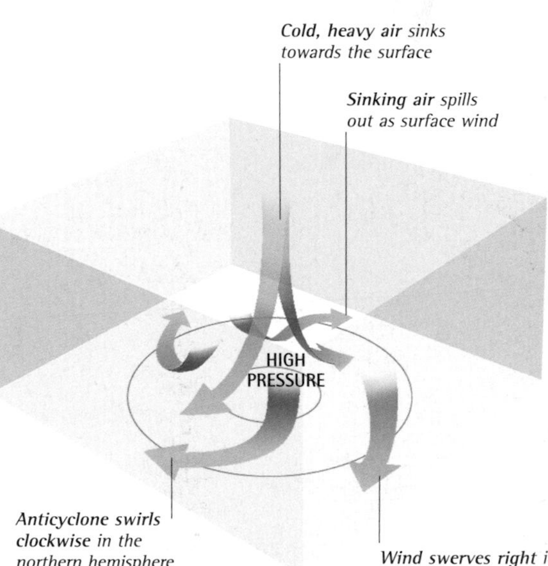

▲ BLUE SKIES
In a high-pressure anticyclone, cool, dense air is sinking. This generally stops warm, moist air rising and forming clouds. So the sky is often clear blue, or with just a few small clouds. In summer, this results in sunny, hot weather during the day, and sometimes low night-time temperatures. In winter, the weather in a high-pressure zone can be just as sunny, but very cold. But sometimes moist air in a high-pressure zone forms sheets of low grey cloud known as "anticyclonic gloom".

Barometer scale shows pressure *in both millibars and inches of mercury*

◄ BAROMETER
Air pressure changes as weather systems move overhead. If the pressure starts to fall, this often means that bad weather is on the way. We measure air pressure with an instrument called a barometer, which gives the pressure in millibars (mb). The average global air pressure at sea level is 1013 mb. The pressure at the core of a high may be 1030 mb, while the pressure in a low could be 990 mb. But in practice it is the relative pressure that is important. A pressure of 1000 mb could be either a high or a low, depending on the pressure in the surrounding area.

A LOW-PRESSURE VORTEX

In the northern hemisphere, air that is being drawn into a low-pressure zone tends to swerve off to the right, because of the Coriolis effect. But the moving air is also being pulled towards the centre of the zone by the core of low pressure. This counters the Coriolis effect, and draws the airflow into an anticlockwise spiral, called a vortex. In the southern hemisphere, everything is reversed, and so the vortex spins clockwise.

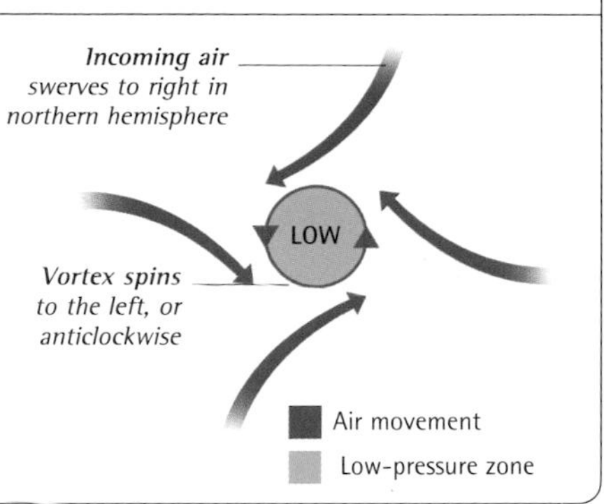

CLOUDS AND RAIN ►
The rising air in a low-pressure zone can carry water vapour up to heights where it cools and forms clouds. So the sky in a low-pressure zone tends to be cloudy and grey, and there is often rain or snow. As the Sun is covered by cloud, the days are relatively cool and the nights can be relatively mild, compared to the temperatures in nearby high-pressure zones.

▼ THE VIEW FROM SPACE
The swirling cloud patterns in satellite images are nearly always formed by low-pressure systems. High-pressure systems are less visible from space because they have fewer clouds in them. Here, a low centred over Ireland is mapped out by an anticlockwise spiral of cloud. The clear skies over mainland Europe indicate the presence of a high-pressure system.

Air swirls into the low-pressure system as surface wind

Rising warm air reduces pressure at the surface, drawing more air in

LOW PRESSURE

◄ DEPRESSION
A low-pressure vortex creates a system called a depression, cyclone, or low. Air swirls into the system as wind and rises in the central low-pressure zone. Winds in a low-pressure system are usually stronger than those in a high-pressure zone, reaching storm or even hurricane force. Low-pressure systems also tend to move faster, bringing wind and rain with them.

WIND POWER

The air flow that we call wind is actually air moving between a high-pressure zone and a low-pressure zone. Winds blow around these weather systems, swirling out from a high and being sucked into a low. The change of pressure with distance between the high and the low is called the pressure gradient, and this determines the strength of the wind. A small difference, or shallow pressure gradient, creates a gentle breeze, while a big difference, or steep pressure gradient, causes a gale.

The steeper the slope, the faster the skater moves

CHANGING THE GRADIENT

***Small pressure difference** usually gives a shallow gradient*

***Gentle wind** blows down a shallow pressure gradient*

***Big difference in pressure** gives a steeper gradient*

***Fast, strong winds** blow down a steep pressure gradient*

***High and low close together** makes the pressure gradient steeper*

***Steep gradient** makes strong winds blow over a shorter distance*

▲ PRESSURE GRADIENT
You can think of the pressure gradient in the same way as a physical gradient, or slope, such as a ramp in a skate park. If one end of the ramp is only slightly higher than the other, a skater will roll down it quite slowly. But if there is a big difference in height over the same distance, the gradient of the ramp will be steeper and the skater will go faster. Air flowing down a pressure gradient as wind behaves in the same way as the skater.

▲ INCREASING THE PRESSURE GRADIENT
A ramp can be made steeper in two ways: by increasing the height, or by reducing the distance between the two ends. The same applies to a pressure gradient. An unusually strong high-pressure system will raise one end of the pressure gradient, making it steeper. This increases the speed of the wind blowing into the low. But the pressure gradient also gets steeper if a low occurs very close to a high. This change in pressure over a shorter distance also increases the wind speed.

CHRISTOPH BUYS BALLOT

The way pressure gradients influence wind speed and direction was first explained by Christoph Buys Ballot (1817–1899), the founder of the Royal Dutch Meteorological Institute. He discovered that the wind does not blow straight down the pressure gradient, as you might expect. Instead it swirls around centres of high and low pressure. This means that wind blows nearly along the isobars on a weather map, rather than across them.

MAPPING THE PRESSURE ►
On weather maps, atmospheric pressure is shown by isobars: lines joining places where the pressure is the same. If the isobars are close together, the pressure is changing over a short distance, giving a steep pressure gradient and strong winds. If the isobars are further apart the pressure gradient is shallower, giving gentler winds. On this map, widely-spaced isobars over Australia show that the wind is much gentler there than over the ocean to the south.

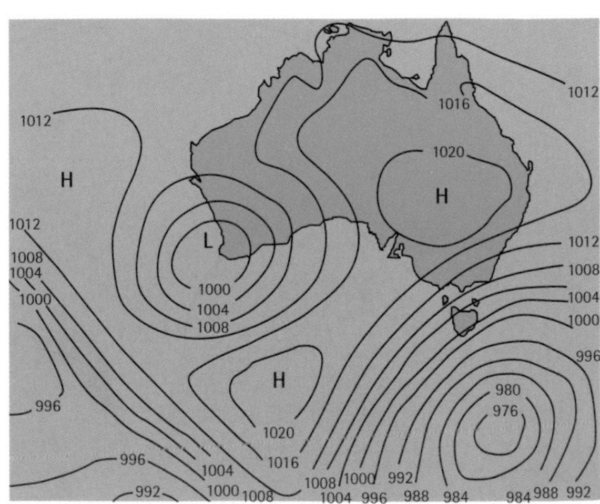

◄ BUYS BALLOT'S LAW
Wind blows around zones of low and high pressure, rather than directly between them. Christoph Buys Ballot showed that, if you stand with your back to the wind in the northern hemisphere, the low-pressure zone is always to your left, while the high-pressure zone is to your right. In the southern hemisphere it works the other way round. This is known as Buys Ballot's law.

WIND SPIRAL ►
In an anticyclone, wind swirls down the pressure gradient in a spiral and spills out at the bottom, rather like someone coming down a helter-skelter at a funfair. In a depression, low pressure makes the air at the centre flow upwards and in the opposite direction, as if the helter-skelter had a system for pulling people back up to the top again.

◄ SPEED AND FORCE
The higher the speed of the wind, the more power, or force, it has. But the wind's force increases at a faster rate than its speed. For example, if the wind's speed doubles from 10 to 20 kph (6 to 12 mph), its force becomes four times greater. At high wind speeds, a small increase in speed causes a massive increase in force that can wreck buildings and trees.

THE BEAUFORT SCALE

In 1805, a British naval officer called Admiral Beaufort devised a scale to help sailors measure the wind speed. The Beaufort Scale is named after him. It ranges from 0 to 12, and covers all wind conditions except the most extreme hurricanes.

BEAUFORT NUMBER	*WIND DESCRIPTION*	*WIND SPEED KPH (MPH)*	*WIND EFFECT*
0	Calm	0 (0)	None
1	Light air	3 (2)	Smoke drifts gently
2	Light breeze	9 (5)	Leaves rustle
3	Gentle breeze	15 (10)	Twigs move
4	Moderate wind	25 (15)	Small branches move
5	Fresh wind	35 (22)	Small trees sway
6	Strong wind	45 (28)	Umbrellas hard to use
7	Near gale	56 (35)	Whole trees sway
8	Gale	68 (42)	Difficult to walk
9	Severe gale	81 (50)	Roofs damaged
10	Storm	94 (58)	Trees blown down
11	Severe storm	110 (68)	Houses seriously damaged
12	Hurricane	118 (73)	Buildings destroyed

WIND AND WAVES ►
Wind blowing over the sea drags the water up into waves. A strong wind creates big waves, and the further they travel, the bigger they get. This means that waves caused by a storm in a small sea like the Mediterranean can never get as big as waves generated by a similar storm in an enormous ocean like the Pacific.

JET STREAMS

A jet stream is a band of fast-moving air that blows around the globe at high altitude. It forms over a large-scale weather front, such as the polar front. There are four major jet streams. They follow wave-like paths around the world, which are constantly changing shape. Jet streams have a big influence on our weather, because they create highs and lows, which they then pull along with them. Unusually large waves in the jet streams are often associated with extreme weather conditions, such as droughts and floods.

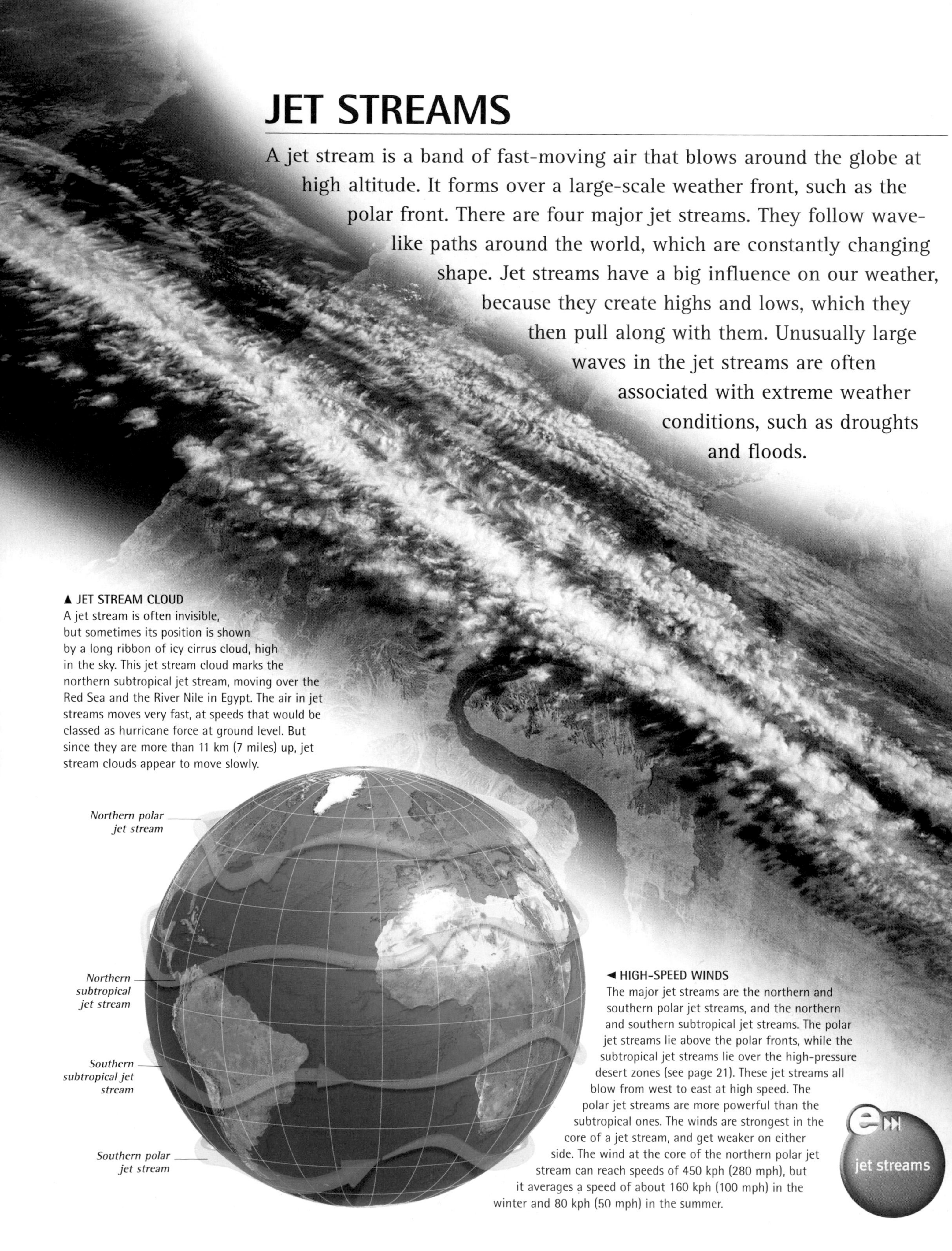

▲ JET STREAM CLOUD
A jet stream is often invisible, but sometimes its position is shown by a long ribbon of icy cirrus cloud, high in the sky. This jet stream cloud marks the northern subtropical jet stream, moving over the Red Sea and the River Nile in Egypt. The air in jet streams moves very fast, at speeds that would be classed as hurricane force at ground level. But since they are more than 11 km (7 miles) up, jet stream clouds appear to move slowly.

◄ HIGH-SPEED WINDS
The major jet streams are the northern and southern polar jet streams, and the northern and southern subtropical jet streams. The polar jet streams lie above the polar fronts, while the subtropical jet streams lie over the high-pressure desert zones (see page 21). These jet streams all blow from west to east at high speed. The polar jet streams are more powerful than the subtropical ones. The winds are strongest in the core of a jet stream, and get weaker on either side. The wind at the core of the northern polar jet stream can reach speeds of 450 kph (280 mph), but it averages a speed of about 160 kph (100 mph) in the winter and 80 kph (50 mph) in the summer.

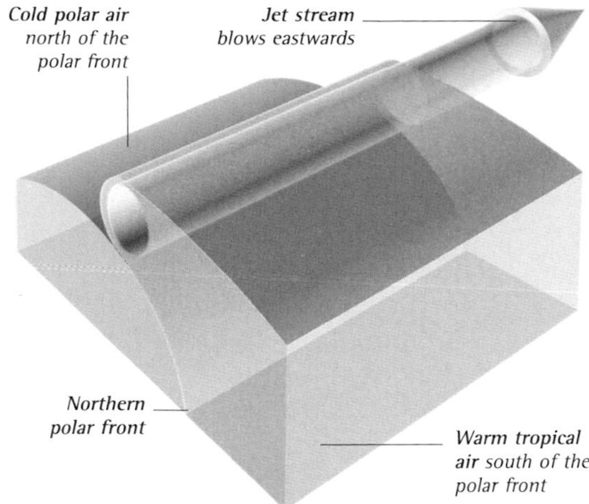

▲ HOW A JET STREAM FORMS
A jet stream develops where warm and cold air masses meet at a front. Near the top of the troposphere, the air pressure is higher on the warm side of the front than on the cold side. This pressure gradient makes air flow from the warm side towards the cold side, and the Coriolis effect (see pages 22–23) makes the air swerve eastwards. The bigger the temperature difference, the faster the jet stream moves. This is why the polar jet streams are more powerful than those over the subtropics.

FLYING HIGH

The jet streams were discovered in the 1940s, by US pilots flying military aircraft at high altitudes. Today, airliners use the jet streams to increase their speed when they are flying eastwards. Flying east across North America with the jetstream reduces the journey time by half an hour. But planes avoid jet streams when flying west, because the fast headwinds slow them down.

◄ RAINY DAYS
The waves in polar jet streams gradually move from west to east, and the weather systems they create are pulled east with them. The depressions develop and deepen on the way, pouring rain on the land below before they break up. This is why regions that lie under the polar jet stream, such as northern Europe, tend to have changeable weather.

◄ SUNNY SPELLS
If the waves in the polar jet stream get very extreme, they can create circulating cells of high-level air that stop moving eastwards. This blocks the movement of depressions from west to east, and often results in long spells of fine, high-pressure weather. Eventually the upper air cells disperse and the lows start moving eastwards again.

◄ DROUGHT
Since the polar jet stream pulls weather systems along, its position affects the weather. A small movement further north or south can make the weather brighter or gloomier. But big shifts in the jet stream's position can completely disrupt the usual weather pattern, causing droughts and crop failures.

JET STREAM WAVES AND THE WEATHER

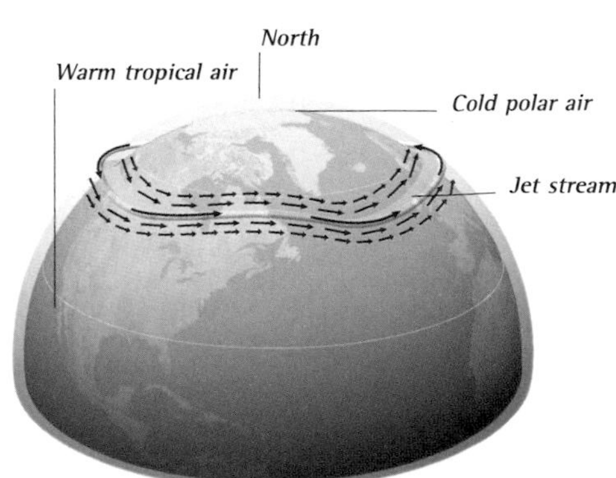

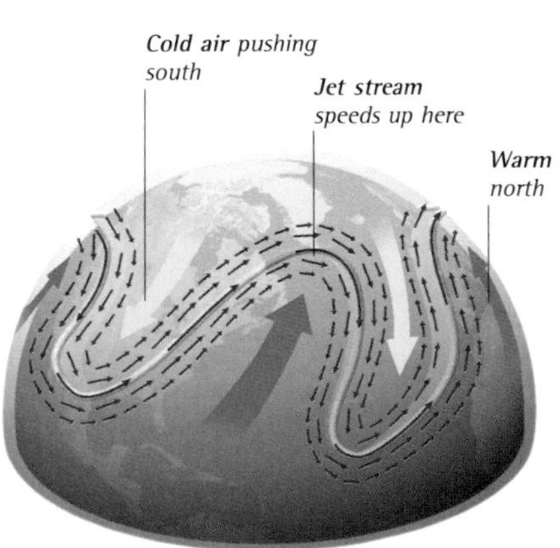

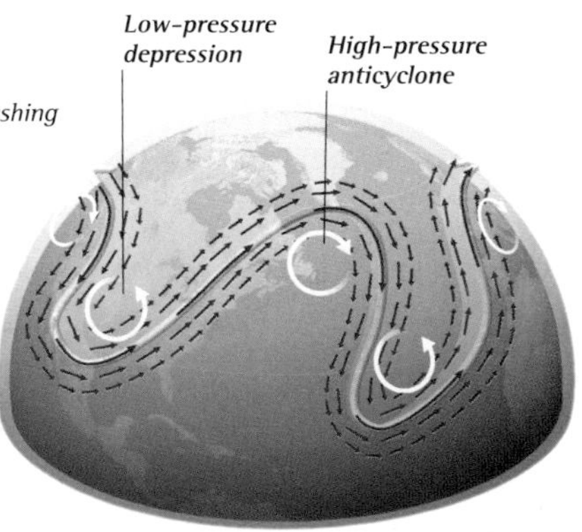

▲ FOLLOWING THE FRONT
The northern polar jet stream lies over the northern polar front. This marks the boundary between warm tropical air moving north from the Equator and cold polar air moving south from the Arctic. The polar front is a moving boundary with four or five waves in it, so the jet stream also moves north and south as it follows these waves.

▲ MAKING WAVES
The polar jet stream travels fastest where there is a big difference in air temperature to either side of the polar front. So it tends to speed up where warm air pushes the greatest distance into cold air. The uneven speeds disrupt the air around the jet stream, and this can make the jet stream waves become more exaggerated.

▲ PUSH AND PULL
As the polar jet stream turns to head south, it tends to become more intense. It pushes air downwards, creating high-pressure zones. As it heads back north, it tends to draw air upwards, creating low-pressure zones. So the wave pattern in the jet stream creates a sequence of highs and lows in the air below it.

WATER VAPOUR

When water is warmed by the Sun, it evaporates, turning into an invisible gas called water vapour. Water is constantly evaporating from oceans, lakes, wet ground, and plants, even when the air temperature is quite low. Water vapour rises into the air, where it may cool and turn back into droplets of liquid water. This is called condensation. This cycle of evaporation and condensation leads to the formation of clouds, rain, and snow. It also absorbs and releases energy that helps to power the weather.

▲ EVAPORATING OCEANS
In the tropics, the intense heat of the Sun raises the temperature of water at the surface of the ocean to well above 25°C (77°F). This means that water is continually evaporating from the ocean, and huge volumes of water vapour are rising into the air. Since the vapour is invisible, it cannot be seen as it forms and the sky is often clear blue. But if the moist air is carried over large, high islands in the ocean, the vapour condenses, forming big clouds that pour rain on to the land below.

MEASURING HUMIDITY

The amount of water vapour that air contains is called its humidity. Air temperature has to be taken into account when humidity is measured, because warm air can hold more water vapour than cold air. The humidity is therefore given as a percentage of the total amount of vapour that air at a particular temperature can hold. It is measured with a hygrometer, which consists of two thermometers. One is used to measure air temperature. The other is kept wet. Air humidity controls the rate at which water evaporates from the wet thermometer, affecting its reading. The two readings are used together to calculate the humidity.

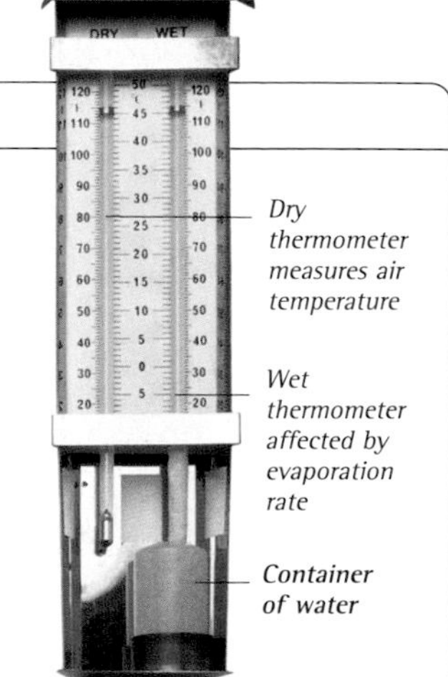

▲ STICKY HEAT
We can't see water vapour, but we can feel high humidity in the air. It is most noticeable in warm weather. This is partly because warm air can hold more water vapour than cold air, but also because the high humidity stops sweat evaporating easily. Sweating is the body's way of losing heat, so if sweat doesn't evaporate, you heat up. The result is the hot, sticky feeling that you get in tropical climates, or sometimes before a thunderstorm.

▲ MIST AND CLOUDS
Even warm, tropical air has a limit to the amount of water vapour that it can hold. When it reaches this limit it is said to be saturated, with 100 per cent humidity. Cold air cannot hold as much water vapour as warm air, so if saturated air cools, the water vapour turns back into liquid water. It condenses into microscopic, but visible, water droplets that are suspended in the air as mist. If the vapour rises into the sky before it condenses, it forms clouds.

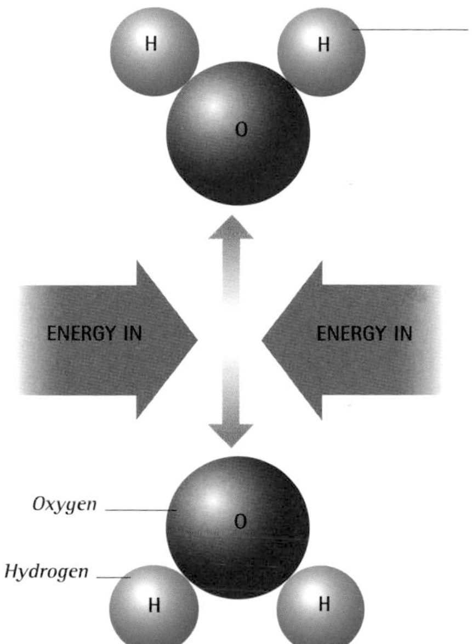

◄ EVAPORATION
When liquid water evaporates to form a gas, its molecules become detached from each other. To do this, the molecules must overcome the forces that hold them together, and this requires energy. They absorb the energy from the air around them in the form of heat. This heat transfer makes the surrounding air cool down, but the water vapour does not warm up because the energy is absorbed by the evaporation process itself.

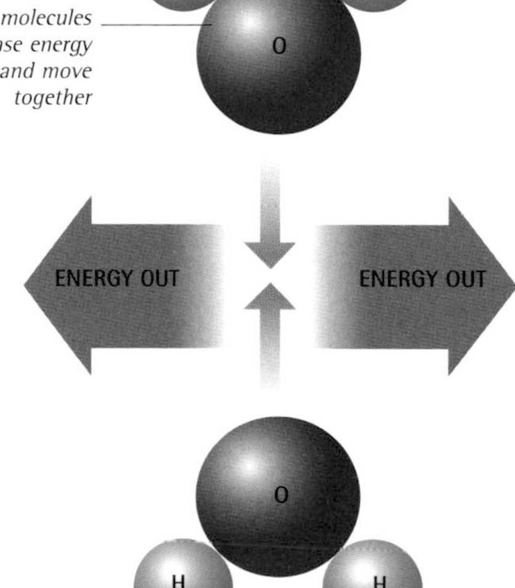

◄ CONDENSATION
Water vapour absorbs energy when it forms, so it contains more energy than liquid water. If the vapour condenses back into water droplets, the energy is released in a form called latent heat. This heat warms the air around the water droplets, making it expand. The air then rises, carrying the water droplets with it. This process fuels the upward growth of clouds, and contributes to the build-up of storms and hurricanes.

▲ MORNING DEW
One example of water vapour condensing from the air is dew. This forms during cool, clear nights, when the heat of the day escapes into space. The air at ground level then cools, water vapour in this air condenses, and liquid water appears on cold grass and other surfaces as droplets of dew. Something similar happens when a cold drink is poured into a glass. The glass chills the air around it, and water vapour condenses on the outside.

▲ FROST
In winter, temperatures at ground level can fall so low that airborne water vapour turns directly into ice, without first condensing into liquid water. It forms the soft white crystals that we call frost. These crystals can build up in such thick layers that they look like snow, but they can also form delicate, branching patterns, especially on glass. When they melt, they often turn directly back into water vapour, "steaming" in the sunlight.

CLOUD FORMATION

When air containing water vapour rises into the sky, it cools. Cold air cannot hold as much water vapour as warm air, so the vapour starts to condense into liquid water. It forms a mass of microscopic water droplets that becomes visible as a cloud. If the air is already almost saturated with water vapour, this happens at low altitude, forming low-level clouds. If not, the vapour-loaded air may rise high into the sky before clouds form. At high altitudes, the air temperature is below freezing point, so the vapour condenses into tiny ice crystals.

▲ STABLE AIR
As warm air rises, it starts to cool. In clear air, it cools by about 1°C for every 100 m it rises (1°F for every 182 ft). This change of temperature with height is known as the lapse rate. As air cools, it gets denser. Eventually it reaches a point where it has the same density as the surrounding air, so it stops rising. The air is then described as stable. As the air cools, the water vapour it contains may condense to form small, shallow clouds.

CONDENSATION NUCLEI

Water vapour has difficulty condensing to form droplets of liquid water unless it has something solid to cling to. In the air, it attaches to microscopic specks of dust, or salt particles formed from ocean spray. These particles are known as condensation nuclei. Air usually contains 50–500 condensation nuclei per cubic centimetre (800–8,000 per cubic inch).

UNSTABLE AIR ►
When a mass of warm, moist air rises, expands, and then cools, water vapour in the air condenses. This releases latent heat (see page 39). The heat warms the air mass a little and, if this makes it warmer and less dense than the surrounding air, it rises further. If the air still contains water vapour, this condenses and releases more heat, and so the process continues. The rising air is known as unstable air.

▼ CLOUD DROPLETS
Typical cloud droplets are about 0.01 mm (0.0004 in) across – so tiny that it takes a million of them to make one raindrop. The ice crystals that occur at high altitudes are just as small. They weigh so little that they are held up by currents of rising air, and float in the sky as clouds. But as more water vapour condenses, the cloud droplets join together and eventually they may fall as rain.

Big quarter circle represents an average raindrop – 1 million times bigger than a cloud droplet (not to scale)

CONVECTIVE CLOUDS ►

Clouds can be formed when moist air is warmed up and then rises. The upward movement is caused by the Sun warming the surface of the ground or sea, which in turn warms the air above it. Clouds then form higher up, where the air is cooling. This process is called convection, and clouds formed in this way are known as convective clouds. They range from fluffy-looking cumulus to giant storm clouds.

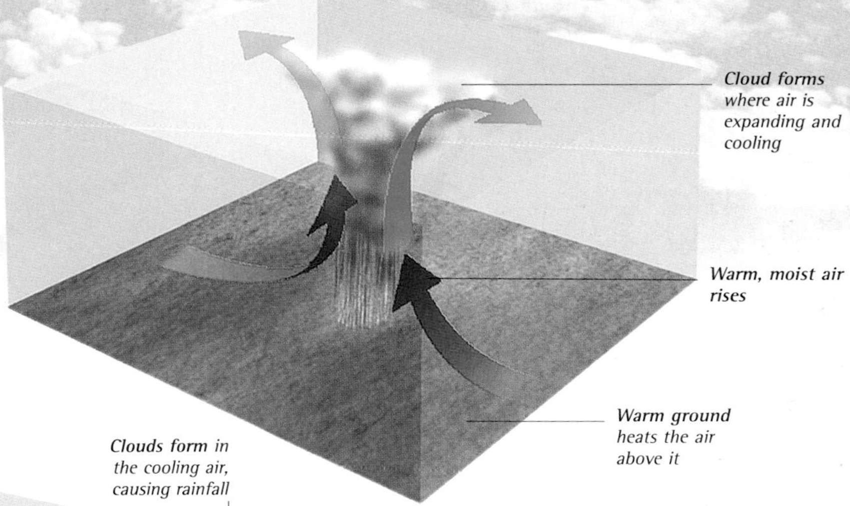

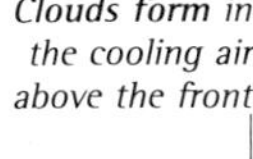

◄ OROGRAPHIC CLOUDS

Air that moves over hills or mountains is forced upwards by the sloping ground. As it rises, it expands and cools, causing clouds to form over the slopes and peaks. These clouds may be carried away by the wind, or evaporate as the air descends on the other side. But new cloud keeps forming, so the cloud often appears to stay in one place as a cap of cloud around the peak. This is called orographic cloud.

Dry air descends on far side of the ridge

Clouds form in the cooling air, causing rainfall

Slope facing away from the wind is often dry

Moist air is pushed up as it flows over a mountain ridge

Slope facing the wind is often wet and green

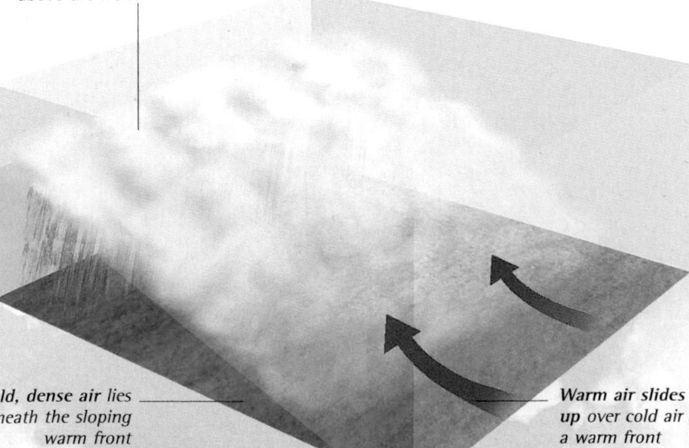

▲ FRONTAL CLOUDS

When a warm and a cold air mass meet at a front, warm air tends to slide up over denser cold air, or be pushed up by it (see pages 30–31). As the air rises it expands, then cools and becomes denser, causing water vapour to condense into clouds. These are known as frontal clouds. Fronts can extend over large areas, so frontal clouds often fill the sky and completely obscure the Sun.

Water vapour condenses into cloud at the crest of a wave

WAVE CLOUDS ▲

When air rises over a mountain ridge, it doesn't always simply sink down the other side. It may carry on rising and falling, in a long series of shallow waves that extend well beyond the ridge. Sometimes these waves are marked by clouds that form at the crest of each wave, known as wave clouds. As the air rises to the crest of a wave, it cools, and water vapour condenses to form a band of visible white cloud. When the air sinks into the trough between the waves, it warms up and the cloud droplets evaporate into invisible water vapour, revealing blue sky.

HIGH-LEVEL CLOUDS

When water vapour rises high into the air before it condenses, it forms wispy-looking clouds that are made entirely of tiny ice crystals. These high-level clouds occur at altitudes of 6,000–14,000 m (20,000–46,000 ft), near the top of the troposphere. They all have names that come from from the Latin word *cirrus*, which means "hair". There are three main types of high-level cloud – cirrus, cirrocumulus, and cirrostratus.

BASIC CLOUD CLASSIFICATION

The names that we use for clouds were devised by Luke Howard (1772–1864), an English amateur meteorologist. He divided clouds into four main types, giving them Latin names: *cirrus, cumulus, stratus,* and *nimbus*. These names – which mean "wispy", "heaped", "flat", and "rainy" – can be combined. A nimbostratus cloud, for example, is a flat raincloud. But "cirrus" or "cirro" has also come to mean a high-level cloud, made of ice. Clouds are also classified as high-, mid-, or low-level, according to the height at which the cloud base (the bottom of the cloud) most often occurs.

NAME	*MEANING*	*TYPE OF CLOUD*
Cirrus	Latin word for "hair"	Wispy or high
Cumulus	Latin word for "pile"	Heaped
Stratus	Latin word for "layer"	Flat sheets

▲ CIRRUS
Cirrus is the basic type of high-level cloud. High-level wind pulls the wisps of cirrus cloud into shapes that are sometimes called mares' tails. These can be almost straight, curved, or hooked and generally show the wind direction at high altitude. Cirrus clouds are nearly always brilliant white and they stay white for longer than other clouds at sunset. Dense cirrus can look grey if it is seen against the light. Although cirrus always forms in dry air, when it develops at the high, leading edge of a warm front, it can indicate the approach of a low-pressure system. Cirrus is sometimes associated with effects such as haloes (see page 55).

TYPES OF CIRRUS

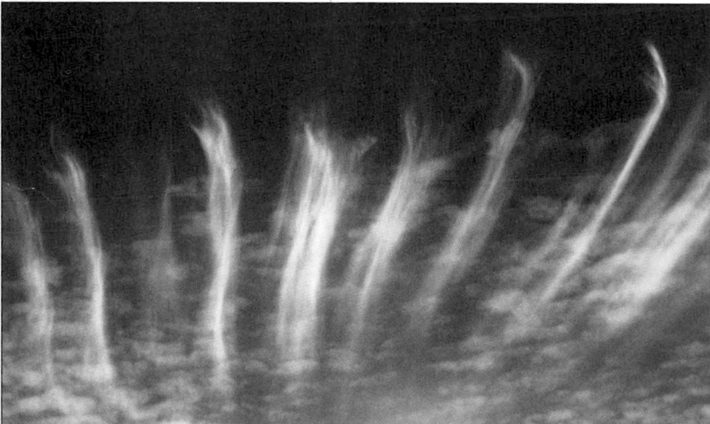

CIRRUS VIRGA
Ice crystals can often be seen falling out of cirrus clouds. These fallstreaks are known as virga. They are forms of precipitation, like rain or snow, but they fall from such a high altitude that they evaporate before they reach the ground. The streaks can give the cloud a ragged appearance, but usually they are swept by the wind into hook-shapes that trail off downwind, but still at high altitude. The longer the trails, the stronger the high-level wind. The long streaks of cirrus virga clouds can sometimes be mistaken for aircraft contrails (see opposite). Virga can also fall from other types of high-level, mid-level, and low-level cloud.

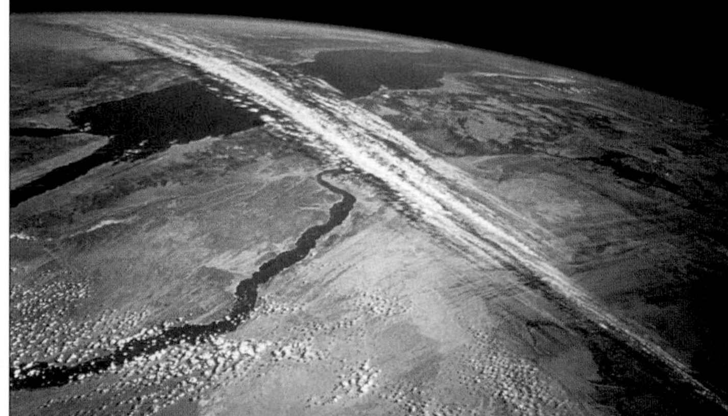

JET STREAM CIRRUS
The positions of the jet streams (see pages 36–37) are sometimes marked by bands of cirrus cloud. These clouds follow the direction of the jet stream's airflow. They show up as very distinctive features in satellite cloud images, as in this picture of the northern subtropical jet stream over Africa. Jet stream cirrus can also be seen from the ground, despite being some 11 km (7 miles) high. It usually takes the form of several parallel bands of cloud. Each band is often made up of short crosswise streaks of cloud, called billows. These are created by the interaction of the fast-moving jet stream with the slower-moving air around it.

▲ CIRROCUMULUS

Rippled patterns of tiny cloudlets at high level are called cirrocumulus clouds. Like all high-level clouds, they are made of ice crystals because the air temperature at high altitude is below freezing point. But air movements have caused the air to rise and sink in regular waves within the cloud. Where it sinks, some of the ice crystals turn into invisible water vapour. This transforms the continuous sheet of cloud into many small cloudlets, which often cover large patches of sky.

▲ CIRROSTRATUS

When high-altitude cloud covers the sky as a continuous sheet, it is called cirrostratus. It can turn the sky white by day and red at sunset. In this picture, cirrostratus forms the sheet of cloud at the top. Cirrostratus is so thin that the Sun or Moon is clearly visible through it. If cirrostratus is forming from cirrus clouds, it often means that bad weather is coming. If it is breaking up, it means that the weather is improving.

▲ MACKEREL SKY

Cirrocumulus and altocumulus (a similar mid-level cloud – see page 44) can develop a regular striped pattern, seen here high above patches of altocumulus. The pattern looks like the stripes on the back of a mackerel, so it is known as a mackerel sky. This pattern is actually more common with altocumulus, which is a more solid-looking form of cloud than its high-level counterpart. The appearance of a mackerel sky is often a sign that a low-pressure weather system is on its way, bringing more extensive, deeper cloud, and rain.

▲ CONTRAILS

The jet engines of aircraft flying at high altitude leave trails of water vapour across the sky. The vapour turns into ice before it has time to disperse, forming condensation trails, known as contrails. The short time that the vapour takes to freeze accounts for the gap between the aircraft itself and the start of the trail. Contrails often have a lumpy appearance beneath, created by air currents from the aircrafts' wings. They can spread widely across the sky, especially on busy air routes, and as they spread they often look like natural cirrus.

MID-LEVEL CLOUDS

Clouds with bases that lie at a height of 2,000–6,000 m (6,500–20,000 ft) are known as mid-level clouds. The highest of them occur in the tropics, where the top of the troposphere is highest. Many mid-level clouds have names that begin with "alto", such as altostratus. Confusingly, this comes from the Latin word *altus*, meaning "high", even though these are not high-level clouds. There are three main types of mid-level cloud: altocumulus, altostratus, and nimbostratus – a cloud type that can also occur at low level.

clouds

ALTOCUMULUS ▲
Large, broken sheets of small, puffy clouds that drift across the sky at mid-level are called altocumulus. This cloud is mostly composed of water droplets, giving it a sharp outline. It usually develops in a layer of moist air where the air currents are moving in shallow waves, and the clouds form at the wave peaks. Altocumulus often forms at night and breaks up in the morning.

TYPES OF ALTOCUMULUS

PARALLEL ROLLS
Altocumulus cloud often occurs at the boundary between two layers of air with different temperatures and humidities that are moving in different directions and at different speeds. The boundary can take the form of large waves. As air rises at the peaks of the waves, the water vapour in it cools and condenses into visible cloud. As it sinks into the troughs between the waves, the cloud evaporates into invisible water vapour, leaving a line of clear sky. This creates parallel rolls of altocumulus clouds, with clear sky visible between them. When the rolls are closer together, the clouds form a type of mackerel sky.

ALTOCUMULUS LENTICULARIS
If air rises up over a mountain ridge and then sinks down on the other side, it creates waves in the air currents. At the tops of these waves the air is cooler, so water vapour condenses and creates clouds. They are called altocumulus lenticularis. The name means "lens-shaped" altocumulus, but these clouds can be a much more complicated shape than this suggests. They often consist of several layers that look like a stack of plates or cushions. These unusually shaped clouds are probably responsible for many reports of flying saucers and other unidentified flying objects.

ALTOCUMULUS CASTELLANUS
As water vapour condenses to form altocumulus clouds, it releases energy that warms the air inside the cloud (see page 40). This warm air rises, making the clouds build up into towering, castlelike shapes, called altocumulus castellanus. This type of cloud is a sign of strong upcurrents in the air. Upcurrents like these may eventually result in the creation of much larger cumulonimbus clouds, which can cause thunderstorms and hail. So although altocumulus castellanus looks attractive, its appearance is often a sign that stormy weather will arrive within the next few hours.

VISIBLE RAIN

When rain, snow, or hail falls from rainclouds such as nimbostratus, it is often visible from a distance as a grey curtain beneath the dark cloud. Sometimes it is lit up from behind by the Sun to give a wonderful silvery effect. This combination of a raincloud and visible rain is known as praecipitatio. The name is the Latin word for precipitation, which is rain or snow falling from a cloud. So a nimbostratus cloud pouring down rain in this way is called nimbostratus praecipitatio. Similar curtains of rain can often be seen falling from other clouds, such as cumulonimbus stormclouds, especially in showery or thundery weather when it is often sunny where it is not actually raining. Praecipitatio is very similar to virga (streaks of ice crystals falling from clouds). But unlike virga – which evaporates as it falls through the air – the rain, snow, or hail in praecipitatio actually reaches the ground.

▲ ALTOSTRATUS
Extensive sheets of grey, or slightly blue, mid-level cloud which often cover the whole sky are called altostratus. The top of this cloud is made of ice crystals, but the lower part is made of water droplets. Altostratus can be thick enough to obscure the Sun, but the light glows through as a bright blur to create a "watery sky". These clouds often form where a warm front is sliding up over cooler air (see page 31). They mark the arrival of a low-pressure depression and often produce drizzle or light snow.

▲ NIMBOSTRATUS
The deepest type of mid-level cloud is nimbostratus. It can also occur at lower altitudes, down to 600 m (2,000 ft), but extends up to altitudes of more than 2,000 m (6,500 ft). It gets its name from the Latin words *nimbus*, which is used to describe rainclouds, and *stratus* which means "layer". So nimbostratus is a thick layer of dark grey raincloud that blocks out the Sun, and produces persistent rain or snow. It usually occurs where a warm front is moving in. Nimbostratus clouds follow altostratus as the front moves over and the weather gets worse.

LOW-LEVEL CLOUDS

Clouds with bases that lie below 2,000 m (6,500 ft) are classed as low-level clouds. They range from the small, fluffy cumulus clouds typical of fine weather, through flat stratus and stratocumulus, to giant cumulonimbus storm clouds that may rise right to the top of the troposphere. Mist and fog that form at ground level are also forms of low-level cloud.

▲ FAIR WEATHER CUMULUS
The white, fluffy clouds that drift across blue skies in summer are called cumulus. They form above rising currents of warm, moist air, at the height where the air gets cold enough for water vapour to condense. Meanwhile, cooler air descends around each cloud and moves in below it, becoming warmer as it descends. This stops cumulus clouds spreading sideways.

▲ CUMULUS MEDIOCRIS
Small cumulus clouds that appear in the morning usually get bigger by the afternoon. This is because water vapour in the clouds condenses and releases latent heat, which causes them to grow upwards (see page 39). They are then known as cumulus mediocris. This type of cloud is more heaped than cumulus, with rising lobes at the top that have crisp, well-defined edges. The clouds have flat bases and usually will not produce any rain.

▲ CLOUD STREETS
Cumulus clouds may form long lines of parallel, separate clouds, called cloud streets. They can form over a strong source of rising warm air, such as an island in the ocean (see page 20), or from air rising over hills, then they trail away downwind. They disperse before they grow too big, and this stops them joining together. Ridges of high land often generate multiple cloud streets.

CUMULONIMBUS

The biggest clouds of all are cumulonimbus, which produce heavy showers, hail, and thunderstorms. Although classed as a low-level cloud, cumulonimbus rises through all the levels, right up to the tropopause, and often spreads out at the top in the shape of an anvil. The clouds may be more than 10,000 m (33,000 ft) high and are made of water droplets at the bottom and ice crystals at the top. Cumulonimbus is formed by the convection of warm, very moist air (see page 41). As water vapour in this air condenses, it releases heat which fuels the clouds' upwards growth.

◄ OROGRAPHIC STRATUS
Sheets of cloud often form in warm, moist air that is lifted over a hill or ridge (see page 41). This forms a layer of orographic stratus that shrouds the peak, such as here at Table Mountain in South Africa. To anyone on the mountain, it seems like fog. A similar effect occurs on high ground that rises into the base of normal stratus, and this is known as hill fog.

▲ CUMULUS CONGESTUS
If growing cumulus mediocris becomes taller than its width, it is known as cumulus congestus. The towering tops of these clouds are brilliant white with a sharp outline, and are often blown sideways by strong winds, as here. The bases of the clouds are frequently grey, threatening, and ragged-looking, which means that they are quite likely to produce rain. If this towering cumulus cloud continues to grow, it will become cumulonimbus.

◄ STRATUS
Extensive sheets of grey, often featureless cloud that form at low altitude, especially in winter, are known as stratus. The base of stratus clouds is rarely higher than 600 m (2,000 ft). Stratus often forms when moist air is carried over a cold surface, cooling the water vapour so it condenses into cloud droplets. This is the same process that forms fog, but stratus is lifted off the ground or sea by air currents.

◄ STRATOCUMULUS
Stratocumulus consists of heaps or rolls of low-level cloud that merge to form extensive sheets. It forms as water vapour condenses in rising moist air. Stratocumulus often occurs when a layer of warmer air above stops the cloud rising further, so it spreads out as a lumpy grey layer. It can also form from flattening cumulus. This type of cloud does not usually produce rain.

MIST AND FOG

If clouds form at ground level, they fill the air with microscopic water droplets that are hard to see through. We call this effect mist or fog. They are essentially the same, but fog is thicker than mist. If objects that are 1,000 m (3,280 ft) away can be seen, the effect is called mist, but if they cannot be seen, then it is called fog. Mist and fog are formed in the same way as clouds – moist air cools until the invisible water vapour it contains condenses into visible water droplets. Mist and fog are often the result of moist air being cooled by cold land or sea.

fog

RADIATION FOG ►
On cold, clear winter nights when there is little or no cloud, heat from the land radiates (escapes) into space. This heat loss cools any moist air above the ground, and the water vapour in it condenses, forming fog. This type of fog is known as radiation fog, because it forms over land that has lost heat by radiation. Moisture is essential to the process, so radiation fog is most common after rain, or in river valleys and wetlands. The fog disappears soon after dawn, when the ground is heated up again by the Sun.

ADVECTION FOG ►
The other main type of fog is called advection fog. This forms when warm, moist air moves over a cold surface and is cooled to the point where water vapour condenses into cloud droplets. Advection fog usually develops over the sea, when the wind blows warm, moist air over cold water. This creates sea fog, which is very dangerous to shipping. Sea fog can also blow inland from the coast, especially at night when the land is cold. It evaporates as the land warms up, but may persist if the land stays as cold as the sea.

▲ COLD OCEAN CURRENTS
Sea fogs often form over cold ocean currents. The fogs that roll under the Golden Gate Bridge in San Francisco, for example, are caused by warm, moist Pacific air blowing across the cold California current that flows south from Alaska. Sea fogs can strip all the moisture from the air, so there is no water left to fall as rain. This effect sometimes creates coastal deserts, such as the Atacama in Chile and the Namib in southwest Africa.

HAZE

Mist and fog are the main causes of poor visibility. But visibility can also be reduced by haze, which is the result of light being scattered by fine dust particles suspended in the air. Haze makes distant objects look paler and changes their colour, and is the reason why distant hills often look pale blue. Haze also causes the reddish effect on the horizon at sunset.

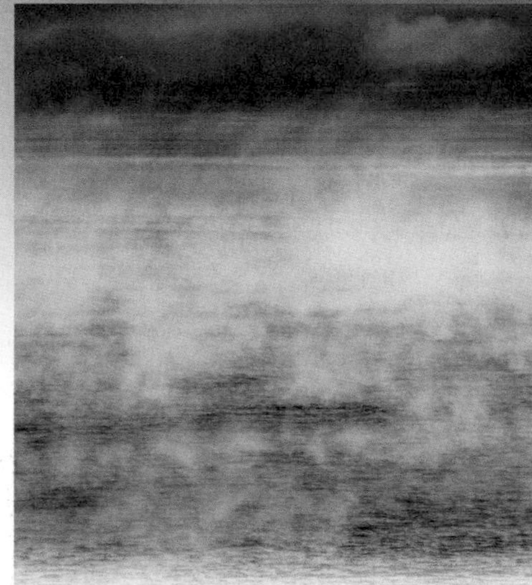

▲ ARCTIC SEA SMOKE

In cold climates, water vapour rising off ice-free water condenses in the very cold air, to form rising columns of visible cloud. Often the water appears to be steaming. This effect is called Arctic sea smoke. It is most dramatic in the polar regions, where the cloud can rise to well above head height before evaporating in drier air.

▲ ICE FOG

If the air temperature is low enough, fog droplets can freeze into microscopic airborne ice crystals. This ice fog is a form of cirrus cloud, but at ground level. The ice crystals glitter if they are lit up by sunlight, so they are sometimes called "diamond dust". Ice fog can also produce visual effects, such as haloes, when the Sun shines through it (see page 55).

▲ FREEZING FOG

In some conditions, cloud or fog droplets can be "supercooled" to below the normal freezing point of water without turning to ice. When this fog comes into contact with cold, solid objects, such as tree branches, it instantly freezes. The layers of ice build into a thick deposit, called rime. This looks beautiful on trees, but can be a serious hazard to road traffic.

RAIN

The tiny water droplets that form clouds can join together to make bigger droplets, that are heavy enough to fall towards the ground. The ice crystals in high-altitude clouds may do the same, joining together to form snowflakes that often melt into liquid water as they fall. Many of these falling droplets evaporate before they reach the ground. They turn into water vapour, which may be carried up in rising air to condense into clouds again. But if they do not evaporate, the droplets fuse together to create big, heavy drops of water that fall as rain.

▲ RAINDROPS
Most raindrops are less than 5 mm ($^1/_5$ in) across, and contain the equivalent of a million or more cloud droplets. Some drops are bigger than this, but they are usually broken up by friction as they fall. Smaller drops fall more slowly than big ones. Any that are smaller than 0.5 mm ($^1/_{50}$ in) are known as drizzle, and fall so slowly that they often evaporate before they reach the ground.

MAKING RAIN

As air rises, cloud droplets grow by condensation until they are heavy enough to start falling. The bigger droplets fall more quickly, overtaking the small ones, which tend to float on the upcurrents of air. But the droplets often collide and fuse to form increasingly large droplets. This process is called coalescence. The deeper the cloud, and the more turbulent the air currents inside it, the bigger the droplets that can form. If they reach a size of about 0.5 mm ($^1/_{50}$ in), they are heavy enough to fall as rain.

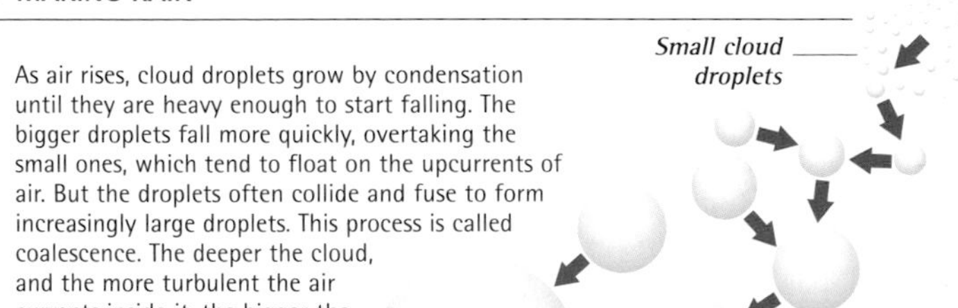

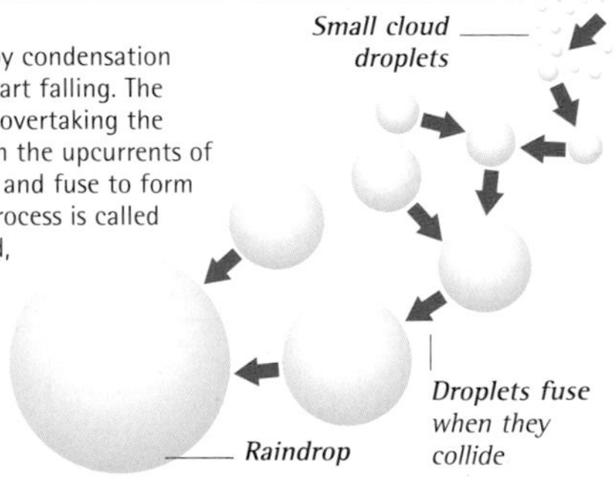

TYPES OF RAIN

WARM RAIN
In warm climates, large cumulus clouds form. These clouds contain no ice crystals, because the air temperature is above freezing. Cloud droplets falling through cumulus clouds coalesce, then get tossed back up into the clouds by turbulence. This forms the big, heavy raindrops of tropical warm rain.

COLD RAIN
Outside the tropics, nearly all rain starts off as ice crystals. These form in clouds where the temperature is below freezing. Very cold cloud droplets freeze on to the crystals, making them grow until they are heavy enough to fall. On the way down, they warm up and melt into raindrops. This is known as cold rain.

▲ PERSISTENT RAIN
In low-pressure weather systems, broad sheets of stratus cloud often form. These clouds are not deep enough or turbulent enough for large raindrops to be made by coalescence. The raindrops that do fall from stratus are often too small to reach ground level. There is often no obvious rain, except on high ground, where it takes the form of a drenching mist of small drops. But stratus cloud may produce drizzle or light rain that persists for hours, because the cloud is so extensive or slow-moving.

HAIL ►
Deep storm clouds generally produce rain in the form of heavy showers, but they can also generate hail. This is formed when ice crystals from high in the cloud fall to a lower level, but are hurled up again by powerful upcurrents. As this happens, they pick up water that freezes on to them. They may do this many times, building up layers of ice until they get so heavy that they fall to the ground as hail.

▲ SHOWERS
Deep convection clouds, such as cumulus congestus and cumulonimbus, produce heavy showers that fall over a small area. The depth of the cloud, and the convection currents within it, allow the raindrops to grow much bigger and heavier than in stratus-type cloud. They sometimes fall in short, but dramatic, cloudbursts that move across country, causing overflowing gutters, flattened crops, and flash floods.

MEASURING RAIN

Rainfall is measured with an instrument called a rain gauge and can be classed as light, medium, or heavy, according to the depth of water collected. Light rain is less than 0.5 mm ($^1/_{50}$ in) per hour. Medium rain is 0.5–4 mm ($^1/_{50}$–$^1/_6$ in) per hour. Heavy rain is more than 4 mm ($^1/_6$ in) per hour. But these measurements can be misleading, because the rate of rainfall is always changing. For example, heavy rain may fall for just five minutes, followed by light rain. But checking the gauge after an hour might suggest a longer period of medium rain.

▼ DISSOLVING RAIN
All rain is slightly acid, because water vapour absorbs carbon dioxide from the air to form weak carbonic acid. The acid eats away at limestone and other lime-rich rocks. This creates spectacular "karst" landscapes with complex cave systems and rocky pinnacles, like these at Guangxi, in southern China. The same process has created the deeply-etched limestone pavements of the Burren in western Ireland, and the underground caverns (*cenotes*) of Yucatán, in Mexico.

Only pinnacles of limestone *are left, due to erosion*

A flat plain *remains where the limestone has dissolved away*

SNOW

Clouds that form high in the sky are mostly made of microscopic ice crystals. The crystals are so small and light that they float on rising air, but they can join together in regular six-sided shapes to form heavier snowflakes that fall towards the ground. These often melt as they fall, but if the air temperature is low enough, they can reach the ground as snow. In really cold conditions, the snowflakes stay separate, but often they partially melt, then clump together to form big, fluffy masses of crystals that fall as snow.

▲ SLIPPERY SNOW
If snow stays thoroughly frozen and dry, it is not slippery. The slippery effect underfoot – or beneath a pair of skis – is caused by the snow melting under pressure. This creates a film of water on the surface of the snow that acts as a lubricant, like oil, allowing the skis to slide easily over the snow.

▼ DRY SNOW
At very low temperatures, and especially where there is little moisture in the air, the small six-sided snowflakes that form in clouds fall separately as powder snow. The flakes are very cold – well below freezing point. All the water in or on them is frozen solid, so the snow is quite dry and does not stick together. It is easily picked up and blown by the wind like dust, as here in Antarctica.

Tiny, dry snowflakes are easily blown away

SNOWFLAKES

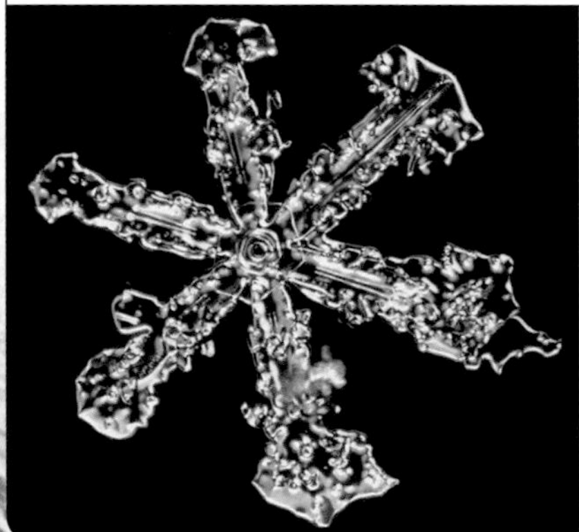

The ice crystals that form in high-level clouds are microscopic six-sided pieces of ice. The clouds also contain water droplets that have been "supercooled" to below their normal freezing temperature. When the ice crystals and water droplets come into contact, the supercooled water freezes and welds the crystals together, creating six-sided, symmetrical snowflakes. Because the ice crystals come together in a completely random fashion, no two snowflakes are ever the same.

◄ WET SNOW
In temperatures that are near freezing point, falling snowflakes are covered with a thin film of water. This acts like glue, bonding them together into fluffy clumps of wet snow. This type of snow melts easily under pressure and then refreezes, so it tends to be more slippery and hazardous than dry snow.

◄ SLEET
If the air temperature is just above freezing, snow can partially melt as it falls. This creates a mixture of wet snow and rain that is sometimes called sleet. The word "sleet" is also used to describe the relatively soft icy pellets that are formed when melted snowflakes or raindrops pass through a layer of cold air, so they freeze again.

◄ SNOW COVER
Once snow has settled on the ground, it is slow to melt. The snow forms a white layer which reflects sunlight and stops the ground underneath warming up. In turn, the cold ground helps to stop the snow melting. But snow contains a lot of air, so it is also a good insulator. This is why an igloo is warm inside, even though it is made of cold snow.

◄ SNOWDRIFTS
Strong winds can pick up fallen snow and blow it around in a blizzard, especially in very cold conditions where the snow consists of loose, dry powder. When the wind blows over or around an obstruction, it slows down on the other side. The snow falls to the ground and collects in deep snowdrifts that can bury houses, roads, and railways.

▲ AVALANCHE
In mountainous regions, snowfall and blizzards can build up thick layers of snow on the mountain slopes. As the snow gets thicker and heavier it can become unstable and, if the slopes are steep, it can eventually slide downhill as an avalanche. The sliding snow often carries lumps of ice and rock with it, so avalanches can be very destructive. Anyone buried by an avalanche is unlikely to survive unless they are rescued within about 30 minutes.

LIGHTS IN THE SKY

White sunlight is a mixture of all the colours of the spectrum, each of which has a different wavelength (see pages 14–15). When sunlight passes through raindrops or ice crystals, the light rays are bent, and the different wavelengths are split up to create colourful optical effects, such as rainbows and haloes. Light that is reflected off dust particles in the air can be scattered in a similar way, producing the vivid colours of sunrise and sunset. Light rays can also be bent when they pass through layers of very hot or cold air, causing mirages.

▲ CREPUSCULAR RAYS
Rays of sunlight can often be seen shining out of gaps in the clouds, or from the edges of clouds. They radiate in straight lines from the Sun, and are separated by bands of shadow. These are known as crepuscular (twilight) rays, because this is when they are at their most dramatic, often tinged with red. Despite their name, these rays can appear at any time of day, radiating downwards in the middle of the day, or upwards at sunrise or sunset.

RAINBOW EFFECTS

RAINBOW
Sunlight shining through rain can be split into a spectrum of colours, from red to violet. The spectrum formed by this effect is circular in shape, but we only see the top half of it. This forms the arch of a rainbow in the sky, always positioned with its centre opposite the Sun. If the spectrum of colours is reflected twice, there may be a fainter secondary rainbow outside the main one.

FOGBOW
The very small cloud droplets that form fog are not big enough to split sunlight into a clearly visible colour spectrum. Instead, they focus it into a mainly white band that takes the same form as a rainbow. Sometimes these fogbows have fringes of faint blue and red. They often form in low-lying sea fog with bright sunlight above, as here over the icy Arctic Ocean north of Siberia.

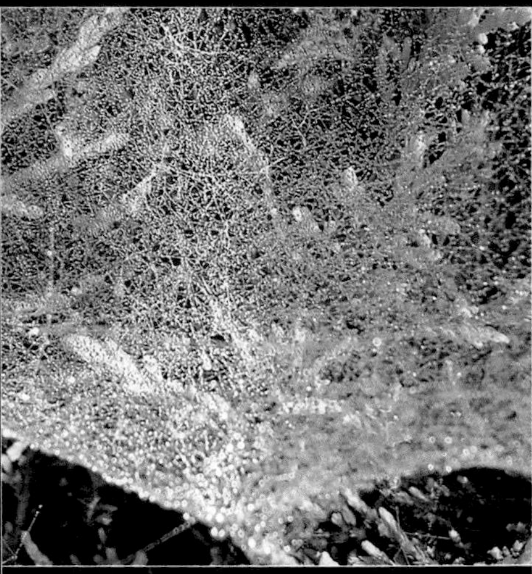

DEWBOW
Dew droplets can produce a rainbow effect, especially in autumn when they are lying on grass that is covered with strands of spider silk. This is called a dewbow, although only a small portion of the bow is ever seen at once. Here light is being bent by dew that has formed on a spider's web, creating a very small dewbow, no bigger than a person's finger.

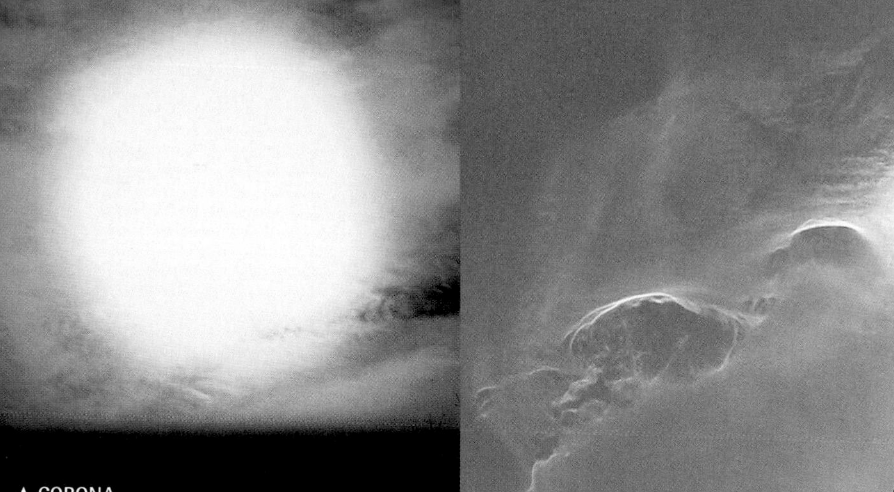

▲ CORONA
When we see the Sun or Moon through thin cloud, it often appears to be surrounded by a coloured ring. This is called a corona. It is caused by light rays being bent, or diffracted, by the cloud particles. These diffracted rays interfere with each other and produce interference waves, which we see as colours. We notice a corona around the Moon more often than a corona around the Sun, because the Sun is too dazzling to look at.

▲ IRIDESCENCE
The diffraction that causes coronas also creates coloured effects in thin, high clouds that appear to be quite close to the Sun or Moon in the sky. Each colour is produced by cloud droplets or ice crystals of a certain size. The effect looks like a paler version of the rainbow colours seen when a film of oil floats on water, and is known as iridescence. We do not often notice iridescence because the Sun itself is so bright, but it can be very beautiful.

▲ HALO
Microscopic ice crystals in the air can bend and split sunlight to create rings of white or multi-coloured light. These haloes may occur around the Sun wherever there are extensive thin, high, icy clouds, such as cirrostratus or thin altostratus. But they also occur near the ground in very cold climates, where ice crystals are suspended in low-level air. In such cases only the upper part of the ring is seen, so these low-level haloes are sometimes known as icebows.

MIRAGE

When light rays pass through layers of air with different temperatures and densities, they are bent. This can make an image of something appear in the wrong place, as a mirage. In a hot desert, for example, the layer of air above the sand is often very hot, but the air above this is cooler. Light from the sky is bent through these layers of hot and cool air, making the sky appear lower down than it really is. This looks like a reflection of the sky in the sand, or a sheet of reflective water, as here in the Namib Desert in southwest Africa. The same effect can be seen on hot roads on summer days.

▼ TWILIGHT ARCH
When the Sun is rising or setting, its light passes at a shallow angle through the atmosphere, and through a lot of relatively dense air. The air scatters all the blue light, so the Sun looks red. Its shape is often distorted into a flattened, wavy ellipse. After sunset, the sky is lit up with a brilliant sequence of colours, ranging from yellow and red to deep blue. This is called the twilight arch.

MOBILE WEATHER SYSTEMS

The weather in mid-latitude regions, such as northern Europe, the northern USA, and New Zealand, is dominated by low-pressure systems, or depressions, that move from west to east. They bring clouds, strong winds, and rain. As a depression moves overhead, its progress is marked by changes in the air pressure and wind direction, and a succession of different clouds. You can track one by watching the clouds and windshifts, and – if possible – using a barometer to check the pressure.

A LOW-PRESSURE SYSTEM ► At the core of a depression is a mass of warm air. As this moves eastwards, the front of it slides up over cold air to form the shallow slope of a warm front. More cold air follows behind, pushing the warm air up to form a steep cold front. The moving fronts are marked by different clouds. Depressions usually move from west to east (left to right in this diagram). If this weather system passed overhead, the first thing you would experience would be the approaching warm front.

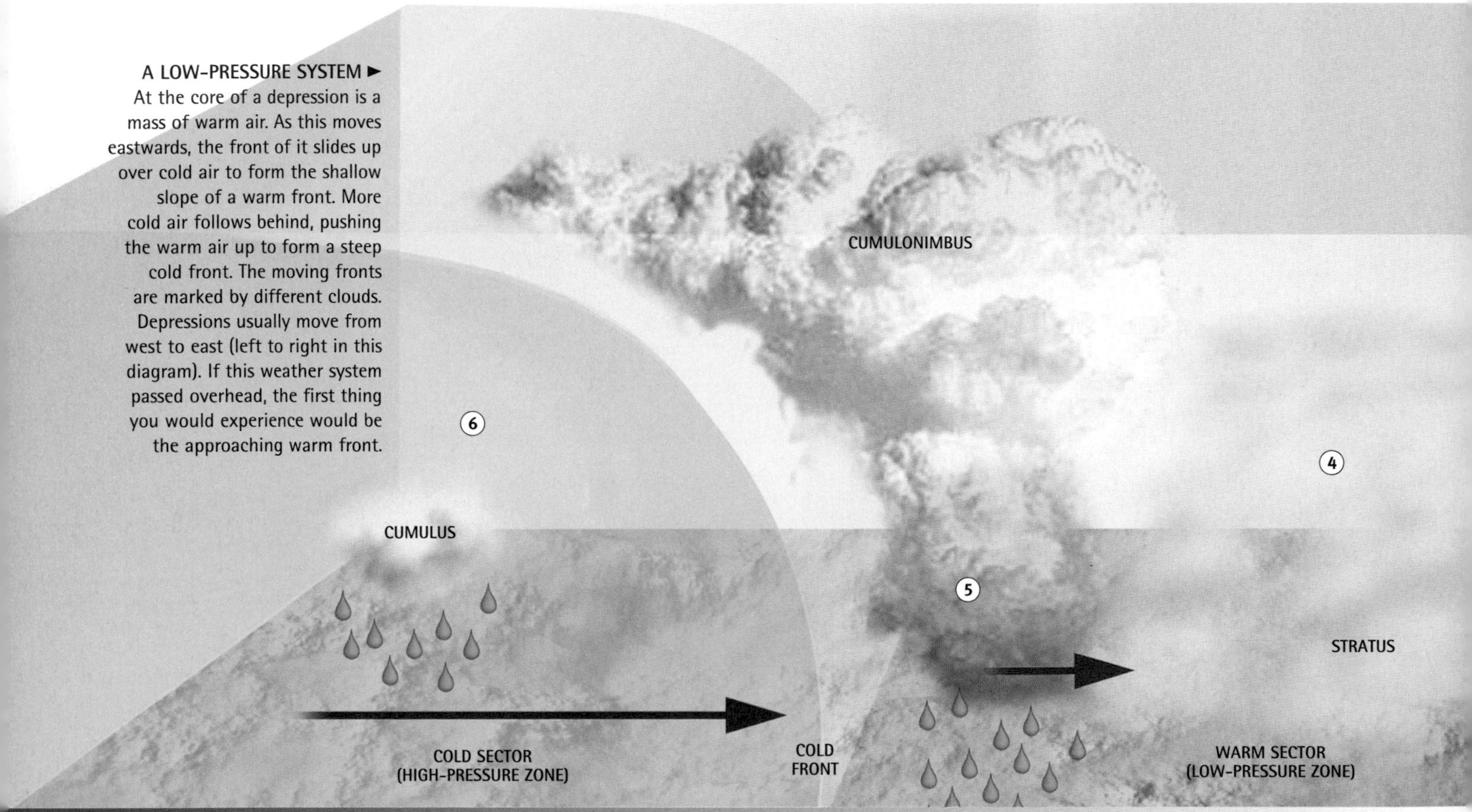

(6) COLD SECTOR
The sky clears in the cold sector as the deep cloud over the cold front moves away to the east. There may be tall cumulus and cumulonimbus clouds and showers behind the cold front. But eventually the rain clouds pass away and the Sun appears, drying out the puddles.

(5) COLD FRONT
As the cold front passes, the air pressure rises and the wind shifts to blow from the northwest (in the northern hemisphere) or southwest (in the southern hemisphere). The moist air of the warm sector is pushed up by the cold front, often creating a band of deep cumulonimbus cloud and heavy showers.

(4) WARM SECTOR
The wind turns blustery as the warm front passes, and starts blowing from the west. The rain often eases, and the cloud base rises a little. The Sun is usually hidden by sheets of grey stratus cloud, but the rain often stops altogether, especially near the centre of the depression.

OCCLUSION

If the cold front catches up with the warm front, the warm air is lifted off the ground. This is called an occlusion. If the warm air is pushed up fast enough, the water vapour it contains may condense, forming towering clouds that produce brief, heavy rain. But this does not always happen. An occlusion is the last phase in a depression, and the skies often clear as the rising air cools and disperses.

VIEW FROM A SATELLITE ►
This false-colour image shows a depression over the north Atlantic, as seen from space by a weather satellite. Low-level clouds are shown in yellow and red, high-level clouds in white. The black areas show regions that are almost cloud-free. The tight spiral of clouds at the centre of the image has been created by an occlusion, and this indicates that the depression is approaching its final stage.

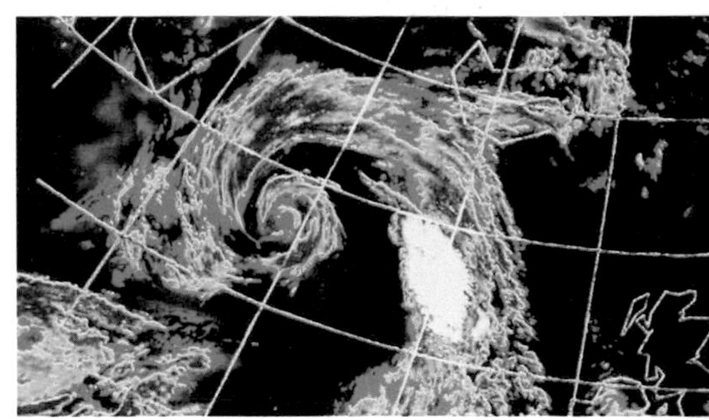

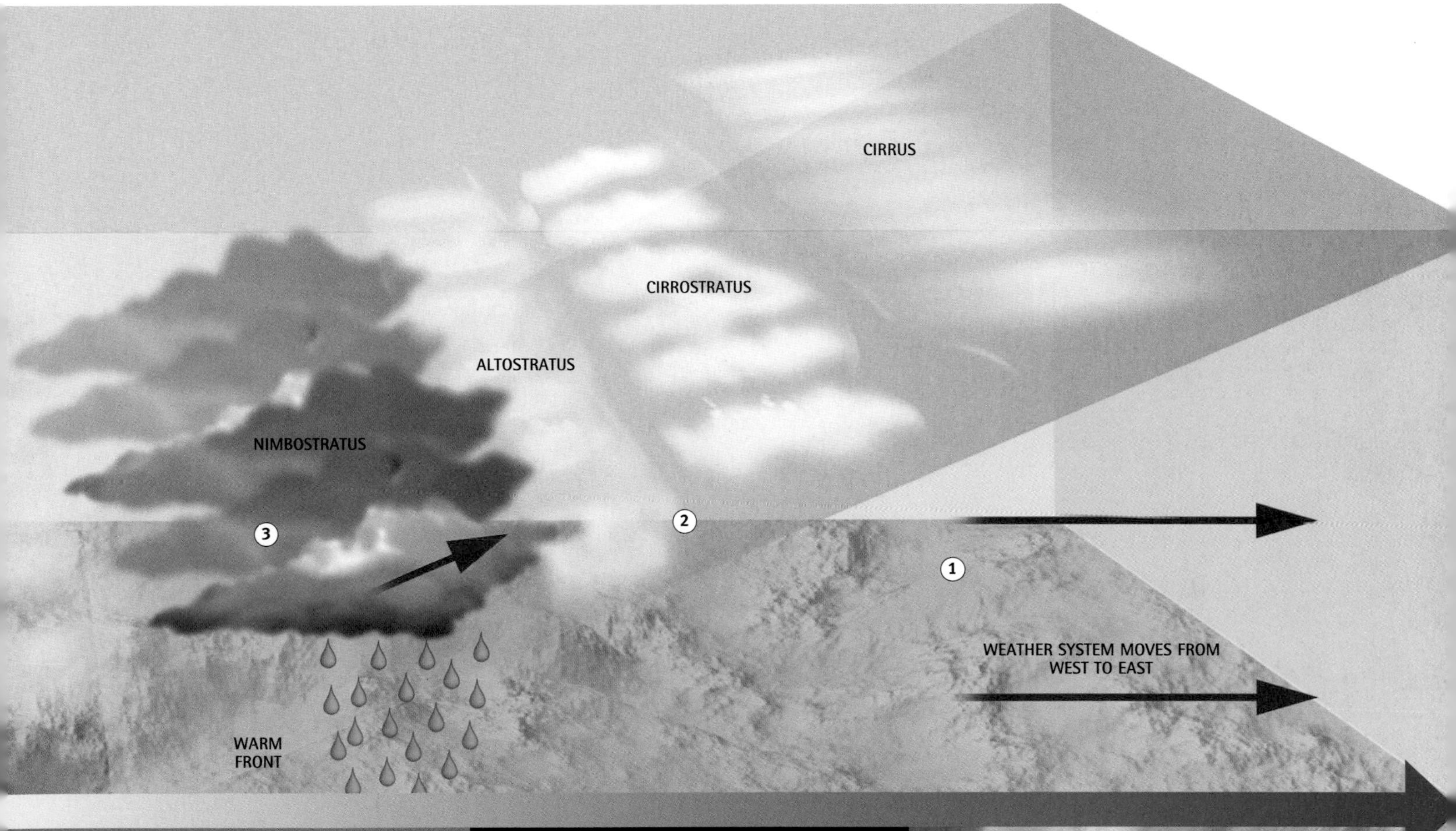

CIRRUS

CIRROSTRATUS

ALTOSTRATUS

NIMBOSTRATUS

WARM FRONT

WEATHER SYSTEM MOVES FROM WEST TO EAST

③ WARM FRONT
As the the front advances, the cloud base gets lower. High-level cirrus clouds become sheets of cirrostratus, and then thicker, lower altostratus. The altostratus builds up into dense, grey nimbostratus, and this produces steady rain that can persist for a few hours as the warm front moves slowly overhead.

② WIND SHIFT
The wind direction changes as the depression passes. Ahead of the warm front, instead of blowing from the west, the wind blows more from the south (in the northern hemisphere) or from the north (in the southern hemisphere), and its speed increases as the air pressure falls.

① APPROACHING WARM FRONT
A mass of warm, moist air slides up over cold air, forming a warm front. Water vapour in the warm air condenses into clouds. The first of these clouds to appear – maybe 12 hours ahead of the front itself – are wispy, high-altitude cirrus. The air pressure starts to fall as warmer, lighter air moves in overhead.

STORM CLOUDS AND HAIL

The heaviest rain falls from huge cumulonimbus clouds, which may be over 15 km (9 miles) high. The immense height of these storm clouds is unique – no other type of cloud is so big. They contain powerful air currents that cause strong local winds. Inside the clouds, these currents toss ice crystals up and down, turning them into hailstones, and generate static electricity that can eventually cause lightning. Cumulonimbus clouds can also create swirling updraughts that may develop into tornadoes (see pages 62–63). So wherever they occur, these giant clouds usually bring severe weather.

storms

DARK THREAT ►
Cumulonimbus clouds are fuelled by heat and moisture. They suck up vast quantities of water vapour from the air, transforming it into a dense mass of cloud droplets and ice crystals. This reflects the light, so the clouds are brilliant white when lit up by the Sun, but very dark and menacing when seen from below. Cumulonimbus clouds often build up in summer when the air is warm and humid, causing the thunderstorms that sometimes break out after hot weather.

◄ CLOUD BUILD-UP
As warm, moist air rises, it expands and then cools. This makes some of the water vapour in the air condense into cloud droplets. The condensation releases energy that warms the air in the cloud, making it billow up (see page 40). As the air continues to rise, the whole sequence repeats. If the conditions are right, this process can make a cumulonimbus cloud grow right to the top of the troposphere. At the top of a cumulonimbus cloud, the water droplets freeze to form ice crystals, and often spread out sideways.

◄ TURBULENT AIR
The air inside a cumulonimbus cloud is very turbulent. Near the centre of the cloud, updraughts of rising warm air may reach speeds of 160 kph (100 mph) or more. Meanwhile, falling rain and hail create downdraughts that spill out from the base of the cloud as strong winds. At ground level, these cold downdraughts cause the violent squalls that often precede rainstorms. Up in the air, the vertical air currents create the turbulence that passengers experience when an airliner flies through one of these great storm clouds.

◄ CLOUDBURST

Most clouds do not survive for long, but a cumulonimbus may take an hour or more to grow to its full height. Then the vast amount of water inside the cloud starts to overcome the updraught, and the cloud droplets begin to fall and join together to form raindrops (see page 50). Eventually, the rain falls in a heavy shower. Big storm clouds can release up to 275,000 tonnes of water in cloudbursts that can cause flash flooding (above).

Sliced in half, this giant hailstone shows its layered structure

Layers are formed by water freezing on to the hail

◄ HAIL

The bottom of a cumulonimbus cloud is made of water droplets, but the top is made of ice crystals. These crystals often fall to a lower level in the cloud where water freezes on to them, but they are then hurled back up by the powerful updraughts. This can happen many times, building up layer after layer of ice. Eventually the crystals get so heavy that they overcome the updraughts and fall to the ground as hail.

MONSTER HAIL

Hailstones are usually about the size of peas. But in some parts of the world, such as the American Midwest, hailstones can be bigger than oranges. These giant hailstones form inside the type of huge storm clouds that can generate tornadoes. The updraughts inside these clouds are so powerful that they keep the huge hailstones buoyed up until they accumulate many layers of ice and weigh as much as baseballs. Then the hailstones fall out of the sky like rocks, destroying crops and smashing windows.

MULTICELLS AND SQUALLS ►

Cumulonimbus clouds sometimes form in a group that grow and collapse in sequence. This is known as a multicell storm. Alternatively, a cold front can sometimes wedge underneath warm, moist air and push it up to create a belt of cumulonimbus cloud called a squall line. Both of these groups of cloud cause high winds, heavy rain, and lightning over a wide area, lasting many hours.

THUNDER AND LIGHTNING

Inside cumulonimbus storm clouds, powerful forces are at work. Vertical air currents toss water droplets, ice crystals, and hailstones up and down, building up static electricity. The clouds become charged up like enormous batteries, reaching huge voltages of electricity that cause giant sparks to leap between the clouds and the ground as lightning. The high temperatures generated by the lightning strikes are so extreme that the air in their path expands with explosive violence, causing the shock waves that we hear as claps of thunder.

CHARGED UP

When ice particles in a storm cloud rub against each other, they lose or gain electrons. All electrons are negatively charged. Particles that lose electrons acquire a positive electrical charge, and particles that gain electrons become negatively charged. The positively charged particles accumulate in the top of the cloud. The negatively charged particles are usually larger and heavier. Most of them settle in the bottom of the cloud.

Losing an electron gives particle a positive charge

Positive particle is carried to top of cloud

Adding an electron gives particle a negative charge

NEGATIVE ELECTRON

Larger negative particle is carried to bottom of cloud

HIGH VOLTAGE ► The contrast between the positively charged ice crystals at the top of a cumulonimbus cloud and the negatively charged water droplets at the bottom is known as the potential difference. It is measured in volts, like the potential difference in a battery, and over the great height of the cloud it may total 100 million volts or more. The negative charge at the bottom of the cloud causes a positive charge on the ground beneath. If the potential difference builds up to more than 10,000 volts per metre (3,000 volts per foot), the electrical resistance of the air may start to break down, allowing the energy to be discharged as lightning.

▼ LIGHTNING STRIKE Air is an excellent electrical insulator, so it takes a huge voltage to overcome its resistance. But once the process starts, a number of relatively faint leader strokes of lightning zig-zag towards the ground. When one of the leaders makes contact – usually with a high point such as tree – it lights up with a much brighter lightning flash, known as the return stroke. Often several flashes occur within a fraction of a second, creating a flickering effect.

▲ THUNDER
The colossal voltage of a lightning stroke heats the air along its path to about 30,000°C (50,000°F) in just a few thousandths of a second. This makes the air in the path of the lightning expand explosively, causing the loud shock wave that we call thunder. This is usually heard after the flash, because sound travels at a much slower speed than light.

OTHER TYPES OF LIGHTNING

CLOUD-TO-CLOUD LIGHTNING
Lightning can occur entirely inside clouds as electricity is discharged from one part of the cloud to another, or between neighbouring clouds. This is known as cloud-to-cloud lightning. It can light up a cloud from inside as sheet lightning, or appear as visible strokes of lightning flashing across the bases of dark thunderclouds.

BALL LIGHTNING
Lightning can also cause strange effects, such as ball lightning. This is a "fireball", up to 2 m (6 ft) across. It descends from thunderclouds at the same time as a lightning stroke, or just afterwards. Unlike normal lightning, ball lightning lasts for several seconds, and sometimes enters buildings.

▲ FLASH AND BURN
The intense heat of a lightning strike can be very destructive. If it hits a tree, it instantly burns a deep scar through the bark to the wood below, all the way to the ground. Lightning strikes frequently start wildfires that sweep through dry grasslands and scrub. They can also incinerate buildings, especially those made of dry wood, unless they are protected by lightning conductors. Lightning can even melt desert sand and fuse it into natural glass, creating branched structures called fulgurites.

***Fulgurite is made of sand** fused into glassy tubes of silica*

e lightning

***Metal rod** leads lightning safely to the ground*

LIGHTNING CONDUCTOR

Lightning is attracted to metal objects because they are excellent electrical conductors. If a metal rod is mounted on the highest point of a building and connected to the ground by a thick metal strip, it channels the electrical energy of a lightning strike directly and safely to the ground. This stops the lightning finding its own way through a more resistant material, such as timber or masonry, and heating it up so much that it is destroyed. The lightning conductor was invented by Benjamin Franklin, the American scientist and statesman who helped to draft the American Declaration of Independence. Before lightning conductors came into general use, tall buildings, such as churches, were regularly damaged by lightning strikes.

TROPICAL THUNDERSTORMS ►
In the intertropical convergence zone (ITCZ) near the Equator, huge amounts of water vapour evaporate from the oceans and rise into the air to form thunderclouds. In some parts of the tropics thunderstorms are an almost daily occurrence: parts of Java have up to 300 days with thunderstorms each year. On this satellite image, the ITCZ is clearly marked by a belt of thundercloud circling the Earth over Indonesia and New Guinea.

Powerful air currents inside storm clouds can cause one of the most terrifying of all weather events – a spinning column of rising air, called a tornado. Violent tornadoes generate the most powerful winds ever recorded – far stronger than the winds in any hurricane. A tornado can rip buildings apart, uproot trees, and flip heavy vehicles into the air. Compared to a hurricane, a tornado affects only a very small area at one time, but it may travel a great distance across country, leaving a long trail of destruction behind it.

tornadoes

TORNADO ALLEY

CANADA

USA

GULF OF MEXICO

Area affected by tornadoes

Tornado Alley

Tornadoes can strike almost anywhere, but they are usually fairly weak. Most violent tornadoes occur in the USA, which suffers about 1,200 tornadoes each year. Most of these develop in spring and early summer in the prairie states of the midwest, an area known as "Tornado Alley". Here, moist tropical air moving north from the Gulf of Mexico meets dry polar air moving south from Canada, causing deep storm clouds that can create tornadoes.

BIRTH OF A TORNADO

THREATENING CLOUD
Fast-rising warm air carries water vapour upwards. The air expands, cools, and condenses into dense cloud to create a big cumulonimbus cloud.

A FUNNEL FORMS
The column of rising air starts to spin. Dark cloud extends down in a funnel. Air rushes in at ground level, carrying dust and debris up with it.

TORNADO
The dark funnel cloud extends down and reaches the ground, creating a full tornado. It may last from just a few minutes to an hour or more.

▼ SPINNING AIR
A tornado may develop from the base of a thunderstorm cumulonimbus cloud if the air in the cloud is starting to rotate. This type of large storm cloud is called a supercell. The wind at altitude blows in a different direction from the surface wind, and this helps to start the currents of rising air spinning. Often a tornado will then extend down from the cloud to the ground below.

▲ RISING VORTEX
Inside a tornado, the air pressure is very low. This acts like a giant vacuum cleaner, which can be powerful enough to tear the roof off a house and suck most of its contents into the air. The winds swirling into the rising air column are also extremely violent – a speed of 512 kph (318 mph) was recorded during the 1999 Oklahoma City tornado. This compares to a maximum windspeed of about 300 kph (186 mph) in a hurricane.

▲ TRI-STATE TWISTER
Individual tornadoes do not last long, but their parent clouds often generate other tornadoes. Multi-tornado systems may persist for several hours, causing widespread havoc. The most deadly recorded was the Tri-State Twister of 18 March 1925, which left a trail of devastation 352 km (219 miles) long through Missouri, Illinois, and Indiana, and killed 695 people.

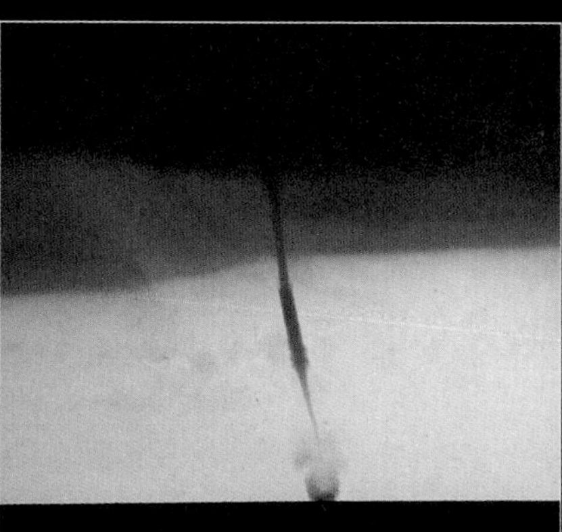

▲ WATERSPOUTS
A spinning column of warm, rising air can also develop over the sea or a large lake, especially in the tropics and subtropics. This is known as a waterspout, because it sucks water up into its vortex. A waterspout is usually less violent than a tornado, but it can capsize boats and even destroy them when it collapses and dumps its load of water.

DUST-DEVILS

In hot deserts, high temperatures on the ground create small currents of rising warm air. These currents may whip the desert sand and dust up into tornado-like spinning columns, known as dust-devils. Most dust-devils only reach a maximum height of about 30 m (100 ft), but a few may be three or even ten times as high as this. They usually last for only a few minutes, because cool air is sucked into the base of the rising vortex and this cools the ground beneath the dust-devil and cuts off its energy supply.

Supercell thunderstorm could soon develop into a tornado

Van contains high-tech monitoring equipment to investigate the storm

STORMCHASERS ►
Some people go out looking for big thunderstorms and tornadoes. They video and photograph them, and simply enjoy the thrill of seeing extreme weather events. Most stormchasers are amateur enthusiasts, but the more they see, the more they learn. The data they collect is now helping the scientific understanding of tornadoes and other violent storms.

THE FUJITA SCALE ►
In the early 1970s, T. Theodore Fujita developed a scale for measuring tornadoes and other high-wind events. The Fujita scale categorizes tornadoes by the damage they do. Reliable wind speed measurements are rare, so the wind speeds given for different F-ratings are only estimates.

F0 64–116 kph (40–72 mph)	F1 117–180 kph (73–112 mph)	F2 181–252 kph (113–157 mph)	F3 253–330 kph (158–206 mph)	F4 331–417 kph (207–260 mph)	F5 418–512 kph (261–318 mph)
Light damage. Some damage to chimneys; branches broken off trees; shallow-rooted trees pushed over; signposts damaged.	**Moderate damage.** Tiles and other surfaces blown off roofs; mobile homes pushed off their foundations or overturned; moving cars blown off roads.	**Considerable damage.** Roofs torn off wooden houses; mobile homes demolished; trains derailed; large trees snapped or uprooted; cars lifted off the ground; small objects blown around.	**Severe damage.** Roofs and some walls torn off brick houses; trains overturned; most trees in forests uprooted; heavy cars lifted off the ground and overturned.	**Devastating damage.** Brick houses demolished; structures with weak foundations blown some distance away; large objects blown around; trucks overturned.	**Incredible damage.** Strong wooden houses ripped off foundations and swept away; cars and other large objects fly more than 100 m (326 ft) through the air; bark stripped from trees.

HURRICANES

A hurricane is a violent, destructive tropical storm. Also known as a typhoon or tropical cyclone, a hurricane revolves around a centre of very low pressure, created by warm, moist air rising off tropical oceans. A hurricane can be over 500 km (310 miles) across, and generate winds of over 300 kph (185 mph). It always develops over an ocean, but it leaves a trail of destruction across any islands and coastal regions that lie in its path. Scientists give each new hurricane a name, starting with the initial "A" and working through to "W".

▲ OCEANIC STORMS
Hurricanes build up over warm tropical oceans, where vast quantities of water are turning to water vapour and rising into the air. The water vapour eventually condenses to form huge cumulonimbus clouds. This process creates a zone of low pressure. Air swirls into the low-pressure zone at low level, then spirals up, forming the centre of the storm, and making the clouds above revolve around the centre.

e ⏭ hurricanes

INSIDE A HURRICANE ►
At the calm centre of a hurricane there is a core of very low atmospheric pressure. The very steep pressure gradient between the core and the surrounding air makes the wind and clouds spiral in towards the centre, with the clouds building higher and the windspeed increasing. A strong updraught around the eye (centre) of the storm creates the tallest of the clouds, which produce torrential rain. They are topped by high-level cirrus clouds that spill out in the opposite direction to the low-level winds.

High-level winds swirl outwards

***Strongest winds** spiral round the calm eye of the storm*

***Low-level winds** swirl inwards*

◄ HURRICANE ZONES
Hurricanes develop only in regions where the sea temperature is above 27°C (80°F). If they move over colder water they die out. But they also need the Coriolis effect to set them spinning. There is no Coriolis effect at the Equator, so the main hurricane zones lie between 5° and 20° north and south of the Equator. Within these zones, hurricanes move west until they strike land. This satellite image shows Hurricane Wilma moving across the Caribbean in 2005.

◄ TRACKING THE STORM
The main hurricane season is late summer, when the sea is warmest. Each storm drifts westwards and away from the Equator until it hits land, then it tends to swerve off in a new direction. This map shows the track of Hurricane Wilma. It formed south of Jamaica and moved northwest to strike land in Mexico. It then veered northeast to head across Florida and eventually fade out over the cold north Atlantic Ocean.

STORM SURGE

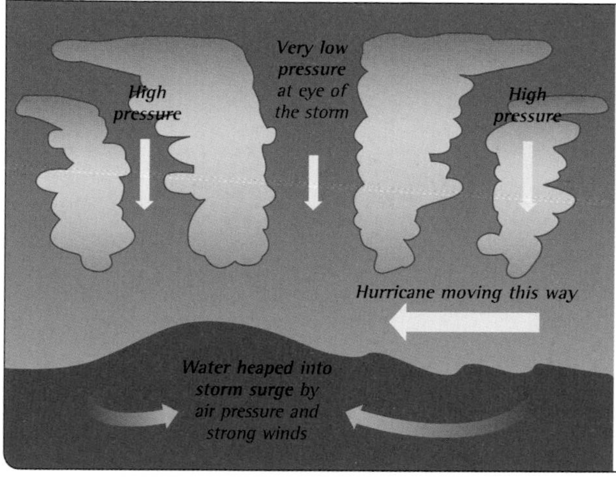

Very low pressure at eye of the storm

High pressure

High pressure

Hurricane moving this way

Water heaped into storm surge by air pressure and strong winds

The extremely low pressure at the eye of a hurricane allows the surrounding higher air pressure and winds to push ocean water towards the centre of the storm. This makes the sea level there rise by several metres to form a storm surge, which is pushed along, ahead of the storm centre. If the hurricane heads towards land, the storm surge heaps up ahead of the storm in the shallow coastal water, creating a wave that may be more than 10 m (33 ft) high. This wall of water can sweep right over a low-lying island or coastline, or flood a coastal city.

Hurricane Katrina blew this wooden house in New Orleans right off its foundations

▲ WIND AND RAIN
Hurricanes are most powerful over the ocean, but they are at their most destructive when they hit land. The combination of wind and rain can do immense damage, flattening buildings and causing flash floods that sweep away whole communities. Hurricanes are graded on the Saffir-Simpson Hurricane Scale, with category 5 being the most extreme. Hurricane Wilma was a category 5 hurricane at its peak, but weakened to category 4 by the time it struck the coast of Mexico.

FLOODING ►
Much of the devastation caused by hurricanes is the result of storm surges. Large areas of New Orleans in the southern USA actually lie below sea level, and the city is protected by sea walls called levees. When Hurricane Katrina struck in late August 2005, the levees gave way under the pressure of the storm surge, and most of the city was flooded. More than 1,000 people died.

DEADLY MUDSLIDES ►
The destructive effects of hurricanes are worse in areas where tropical forests have been cut down. Trees soak up rain and hold the soil together. If they are removed, water can flood off the land in deadly mudslides that do far more damage than the wind. In 1998, Hurricane Mitch dumped 127 cm (50 in) of rain on Central America. The deluge caused many mudslides like this one in northwest Nicaragua, and more than 11,000 people were killed.

MONSOONS

As the seasons change, the part of the Earth that receives the strongest sunlight changes from the northern tropics to the southern tropics and back. This makes tropical weather systems move north and south too. It causes powerful winds that blow in opposite directions depending on the season, carrying wet or dry weather with them. These wind reversals, known as monsoons, dominate the climates of India and Southeast Asia.

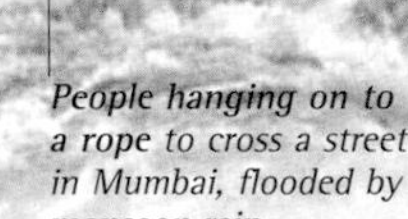

People hanging on to a rope to cross a street in Mumbai, flooded by monsoon rain

▲ MONSOON FLOODING
In a monsoon climate, months of dry weather suddenly give way to months of heavy rain. The people who live in southern Asia depend on the rain to relieve the drought, and turn the parched ground into fertile fields. If the wet monsoon is late, it can ruin the season's crops. But the torrential rain can also cause catastrophic flooding, as in July 2005 when the heaviest rains ever recorded in India turned Mumbai into a disaster zone.

MOVING WITH THE SEASONS ►
The intertropical convergence zone (ITCZ) near the Equator is a region of low pressure, clouds, and thunderstorms. In this satellite image, its position is marked by a belt of clouds extending across the Indian Ocean from Indonesia to Africa. The position of the ITCZ moves north and south of the Equator as the seasons change. As it moves north over southern Asia in summer, it causes a seasonal windshift, or monsoon.

THE INDIAN MONSOON

WET MONSOON
During summer in the northern hemisphere, the Asian landmass warms up and warm air rises over the region to the north of India. This draws the ITCZ north, creating a low-pressure zone over the Himalayas. Warm, wet air from the Indian Ocean in the south is pulled north by the low pressure. Huge clouds form and pour the heavy rain of the wet monsoon over India.

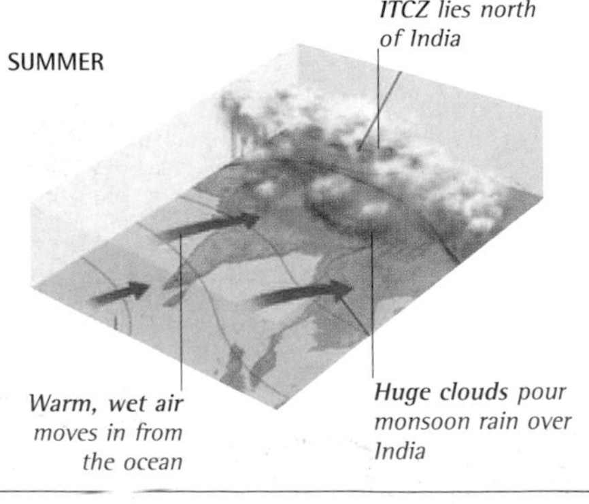

DRY MONSOON
During winter in the northern hemisphere, the Indian Ocean is warmer than the Asian continent and the ITCZ moves south, as shown in the satellite image above. The low-pressure zone of the ITCZ draws cool, dry air from Tibet south over India. So the wind blows in the opposite direction, and causes the long droughts of the dry monsoon.

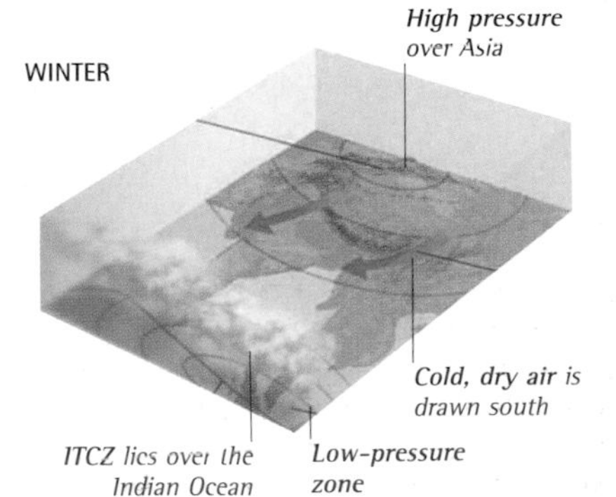

▲ MONSOON FOREST
The seasonal windshifts of the Asian monsoon affect a huge area, extending east from India and Pakistan, through Southeast Asia, southern China, and Japan, to northern Australia. This weather pattern has created a habitat called monsoon forest, the home of the tiger in India. It is similar to tropical rainforest, and has a similar climate during the wet monsoon, but the trees and other plants have adapted to survive the long droughts of the dry season.

▲ FLOWERING DESERT
Monsoon-type seasonal windshifts occur all around the world in the tropics. They even affect the cactus deserts of northern Mexico. The Sonoran Desert, for example, is dry for much of the year, but from July to mid-September a summer monsoon brings wet tropical air and frequent local thunderstorms. The rain makes the desert burst into flower, and gives the spiny cacti a chance to soak up huge volumes of vital water.

DUST FROM THE SAHARA

Seasonal winds also affect the region around the Mediterranean Sea. Low-pressure weather systems that develop in spring draw desert air north from the Sahara. This creates hot, dry winds, known as the scirocco and the khamsin. These winds often carry reddish desert dust in vast plumes, as shown in this satellite image of the khamsin blowing north off Egypt. The winds pick up water vapour from the Mediterranean, and may drop the moisture and dust over Europe as red rain. Similar desert winds include the hot leveche that blows over Spain, and the harmattan that blows over the lands south of the Sahara.

WET AND DRY SEASONS ►
In November, the ITCZ moves over the Serengeti grasslands of East Africa, bringing heavy rain and violent thunderstorms. The rain makes the grass grow. But in June, when the ITCZ has moved north, the rain stops and a long dry season begins. The grass stops growing, forcing herds of grazing animals like these wildebeest and zebra to go on long journeys, or migrations, to find food.

LOCAL WINDS

Many parts of the world experience local winds that are caused or influenced by the landscape, or by the different conditions over the land and sea. Some of these winds blow almost all the time, others tend to blow at certain times of day. Local winds are caused by various combinations of rising warm air and sinking cold air, and the differences in air pressure that these create. These winds can create quite different climatic conditions within small areas, especially in mountainous regions.

▲ POLAR WINDS
Antarctica and Greenland are covered by huge sheets of ice. The ice is thicker in the middle of the ice sheet than at its edges, creating a huge dome shape, which becomes steeper near its edge. The ice chills the air above, which becomes very dense. It spills out towards the coast, flowing downhill in polar katabatic winds that can reach storm force. If the winds pick up powder snow, they create freezing blizzards. It is these winds that make Antarctic exploration so difficult and dangerous.

SEA AND LAND BREEZES

DAYTIME
On sunny days, the land heats up more quickly than the sea. The warm land heats the air above it, which rises. This draws in cooler air from over the sea, in the form of a sea breeze. The rising air cools and flows out to sea at higher level. It then sinks to replace the air that has blown inland.

NIGHT-TIME
At night the circulation reverses, because the land loses heat much faster than the sea. As the land cools down, it cools the air above it. The cooled air sinks and flows out to sea as a land breeze, to replace air that is rising over the relatively warm sea and flowing inland at higher level.

KATABATIC WINDS ►
In mountainous regions, high ground loses heat rapidly at night. The air over the high ground cools and becomes denser, then flows downhill as a katabatic (falling) wind. The cool air may become warmer as it sinks, or it may replace warmer air in the valley below to create a pool of frost or fog. Katabatic winds can be quite strong. In steep-sided Scandinavian fjords they are a hazard to shipping, sometimes blowing almost vertically down on the water.

◄ ANABATIC WINDS

In mountainous regions, the sides of a valley often get more sunlight than the valley floor. As a result, they warm up more during the day, heating the air above them. This warm air rises, drawing cooler air up the slope from the valley to replace it. The result is a light upslope, or anabatic, wind. This is the opposite of the downslope katabatic wind that usually develops at night.

◄ VALLEY WINDS

A valley can funnel a flow of air, concentrating it into a powerful wind. One of the most notorious is the mistral wind, which blows down the Rhône valley between the Alps and the Massif Central in southern France. The wind is drawn south by low-pressure systems in the Gulf of Genoa, especially in winter, and it is pushed along by katabatic winds that occur higher up the valley.

THE FÖHN EFFECT ▼

When moist air rises over one side of a long mountain ridge, it cools slowly and the water vapour it contains condenses to form clouds and rain. The rain falls on the windward side of the ridge. Once the air clears the ridge, it rushes down the other side, becoming warmer as it sinks. As it is now dry, the air warms up very quickly. It becomes a warm, dry wind, such as the föhn in the Alps or the chinook in the eastern Rockies in the USA.

OCEANIC WINDS

Winds blowing over land are slowed down by friction with the ground. Winds that blow over the sea are less affected by friction, because the water surface is smoother than the ground. So ocean winds usually blow more strongly than land winds. In the Southern Ocean, where there is no land to slow the wind, it regularly builds up to near-hurricane force as it howls around Antarctica, and can carry soaring albatrosses vast distances over the ocean.

FLOODS AND DROUGHTS

Heavy rain or scorching heat can have dramatic effects on the landscape. Flash floods or mudslides can destroy everything in their path, while serious droughts may turn fertile farmland to dust. In deserts and monsoon regions these events are a regular, natural feature of the climate. But in other places they strike once in a lifetime. Sometimes these catastrophes are caused by freak weather, but often they are made worse by the way human activity has changed the landscape.

Mature trees uprooted by the flood

◄ FLASH FLOOD
Where water flowing downhill is funnelled through a valley, very heavy rain can cause a flash flood. The water builds up into a torrent that can sweep rocks, trees, cars, and houses away. In August 2004, a flood like this surged down a steep river valley at the village of Boscastle in Britain, after a severe thunderstorm. The deep floodwater washed away buildings and bridges, and carried 80 cars right out to sea.

Wrecked cars buried under heaps of debris

◄ FLOODS
Torrential tropical rain can cause flooding on a colossal scale. In 1988, more than half of Bangladesh was flooded by water carried down from the Himalayas by the Ganges and Brahmaputra rivers. The floods killed over 2,000 people and made 45 million homeless. Just three years later, the country was flooded again and 150,000 died.

DESERT TORRENTS

FLOODWATER
Rare, but heavy, rainstorms in deserts cause flash floods that scour channels through the barren, dusty soil. Every time there is a storm, fast-flowing floodwater loaded with rock and sand pours down the channels, grinding away the rock. Over thousands of years, this turns them into steep-sided valleys, called wadis or arroyos.

DRY VALLEY
When the rain stops, the floodwater quickly drains away or dries out, and the wadis are left dry. Each wadi may stay dry for months, or even years, but eventually another rainstorm will send a fresh torrent surging down the dry stream bed. So over time, the desert landscape is shaped by floodwater, despite the extremely dry climate.

◄ DROUGHT
At the edges of deserts, the dry soil is held together by the roots of grasses and other plants that can survive long droughts. But if local people allow too many farm animals to eat the grass, they can kill it. Without the plants, the soil dries out and blows away, or is carried off by floodwater after rainstorms. So the effect of the drought is made much worse. The land gradually turns to desert, and the people and their animals may starve.

◄ STORM FORCE
Very strong winds in regions that are not used to them can flatten forests. In October 1987, a violent storm swept through southern Britain, uprooting more than 15 million trees and wrecking thousands of buildings. The storm was not as powerful as a tropical hurricane, but its effect on the landscape was just as devastating. The native trees were not adapted to withstand such strong winds, which occur very rarely in northern Europe.

◄ DUST BOWL
If farmers in dry climates destroy the natural plants and keep growing crops, the soil becomes thin and barren. The problem can be solved by spreading organic fertilizer on the land, but otherwise the dry soil turns to dust. This happened in the American Midwest in the 1930s. After years of drought and repeated wheat crops, the area became a dust bowl. Eventually the soil just blew away, in dust storms that swept across America.

MUDSLIDES

Tropical forests are able to survive violent storms, because the trees that grow there have evolved to cope with high winds and torrential rain. The tree roots hold the soil together and help to soak up the rainwater. So regions that still have their natural plant cover often get through hurricanes with surprisingly little damage. But if people cut down the trees and the natural vegetation is stripped away, there is nothing to stop the soil being carried away by floodwater. After heavy rainfall, the soil can turn to liquid mud. It pours down mountain slopes in catastrophic mudslides, sweeping through towns, destroying buildings, and burying people alive.

▲ WILDFIRE
Weeks of drought can dry out a landscape so much that fires break out. They burn most fiercely in regions like Australia, California, and southern Europe, where the plants are full of oils that catch alight easily. The plants can survive small, regular fires, which soon burn out. But if fire control measures prevent small fires, the dead leaves may build up to provide fuel for much bigger, more destructive fires, like this one in Portugal.

ICE

In the coldest parts of the world, air and ground temperatures fall well below the freezing point of water, especially in winter. So a lot of the water in the environment exists in the form of solid ice. Some ice is formed when water in the ground freezes, or the surfaces of rivers, lakes, and polar oceans freeze. The rest is the result of snow persisting throughout the summer, and building up in layers over the years. Eventually, the snow is compacted into the glaciers, ice caps, and ice sheets that form on high mountains and polar landmasses.

DEEP FREEZE

Baby mammoth was too young to have tusks

Chestnut-coloured hair was preserved on the legs

Arctic permafrost can act as a long-term deep freeze, preserving the remains of plants, animals, and even people for thousands of years. The frozen bodies of several prehistoric woolly mammoths have been found in Siberia, including this baby mammoth recovered from near the Kolyma River in 1977. According to radiocarbon dating, the animal died about 40,000 years ago. But its skin, internal organs, and some of its hair have been preserved by the ice.

◄ PERMAFROST
In the polar regions, land that is not covered by permanent ice freezes solid in winter. In summer, the surface of this ground thaws out, but the deeper layers stay frozen. This deep permafrost stops melting water draining away, so it forms pools and swamps that cover vast areas in the Arctic. This type of semi-frozen landscape is called tundra. In places, ice trapped in the soil pushes up blister-like mounds, called pingos, which may be 50 m (160 ft) high.

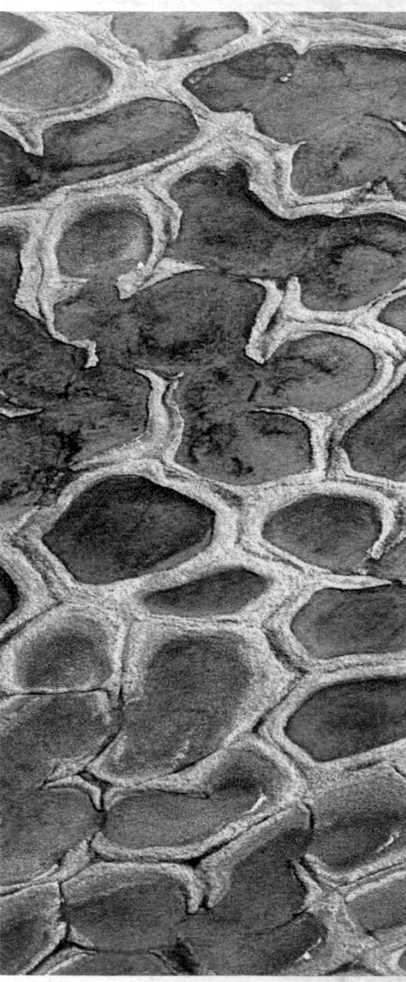

FREEZE AND THAW ►
When water freezes to form ice, it expands. As icy landscapes freeze, thaw, and freeze again with the seasons, the expanding ice forces the rocks and soil apart. This effect can shatter boulders and rocky cliff faces, reducing them to heaps of rubble and scree. It creates patterns of cracks in the ground that gradually enlarge and fill with rocky debris to form tundra polygons, like these in Alaska. Each polygon is several metres across.

FROZEN OCEAN ►
Freezing air temperatures at the North Pole make ice form at the surface of the Arctic Ocean. The ice is quite thin compared to ice sheets that lie on land, and it is always on the move, driven by the ocean currents that swirl around the pole. The polar ice is permanent, unlike the pack ice that forms around its fringes each winter. But it is constantly being replaced, as new ice forms on water flowing towards the pole, and old ice melts away.

GLACIERS ►

Snow that falls in cold polar or mountain regions may not melt away in summer. Over many years, the snow builds up until its own weight squeezes most of the air out and turns it to solid ice. This flows very slowly downhill in a moving river of ice, called a glacier. Eventually, the glacier either reaches an inlet of the sea, as here in Alaska, or its leading edge melts to create a lake or river.

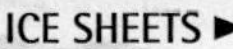

◄ ICEBERGS

Most icebergs are formed from Arctic or Antarctic glaciers that flow down to the ocean. When they reach the sea, big chunks of ice break off and float away as icebergs. If the ice is old enough, it is compressed to a very dense form that is blue. Since glaciers are formed from snow, icebergs are made of fresh water. They also contain rocks and dust that fall to the ocean floor when they melt in the ocean.

ICE SHEETS ►

The vast ice sheets that cover most of Antarctica and Greenland are really huge glaciers. In central Antarctica, any snow that falls never melts, so it gradually builds up as ice. The Antarctic ice sheet is up to 4.5 km (2.8 miles) thick. It buries whole mountains, so that just their peaks stick up through the ice. The ice is so heavy that it has made Antarctica sink nearly a kilometre (0.6 mile) into the Earth.

Pressure ridges are pushed up by moving ice

FREEZE-UP

Serious freeze-ups are not restricted to the polar regions. Winters in normally warmer areas can sometimes be cold enough to make lakes and rivers freeze and to cause destructive ice storms. This kind of cold spell is often caused by a high-pressure system that stays in the same position for days or weeks, and is most common in areas with a continental climate. If warm, moist air is carried over a very cold region, it can result in freezing rain that covers everything with ice. In this photo, taken in Montreal, Canada in the late 19th century, a similar effect has been caused by the water used to put out a fire, which has frozen on the building.

EL NIÑO

Roughly every two to five years, there is a change in the usual pattern of sea surface temperatures over the Pacific. The ocean currents that normally flow from east to west weaken. Warm surface water flows back east, suppressing the cold currents that bring food-rich water to the eastern Pacific. This event is known as El Niño. It coincides with the Southern Oscillation, a reversal of air circulation in the South Pacific that disrupts the weather, causing droughts and floods. The two effects are described as the El Niño–Southern Oscillation, or ENSO.

EFFECT ON WILDLIFE ► The Galapagos islands off South America are surrounded by the cold waters of the Peru Current, which teem with plankton and fish. During an El Niño event, warm water flows east and suppresses the cold current. The plankton cannot get enough nutrients and die, along with many plankton-eating fish. Seabirds like these boobies cannot find enough food for their young, and the chicks starve.

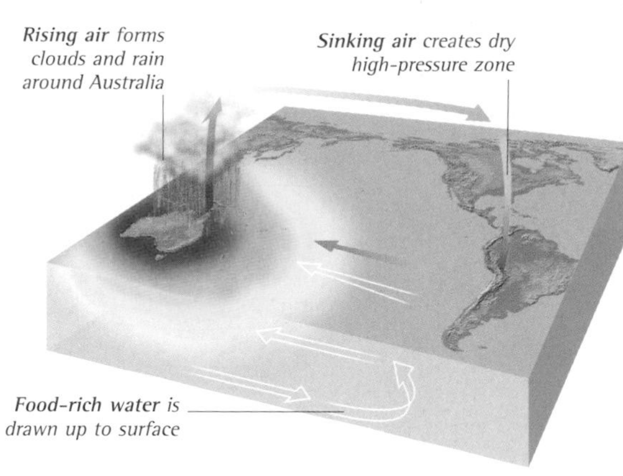

▲ NORMAL YEAR
Normally, the trade winds blow across the tropical Pacific towards the west, piling up warm surface water around Australia and Indonesia. This draws water away from the South American coast, causing cold water to well up from the ocean floor. This food-rich cold water supports a vast mass of wildlife. Meanwhile, water vapour rising off the ocean in the west fuels heavy rain, and forms part of an air circulation pattern called the Pacific cell.

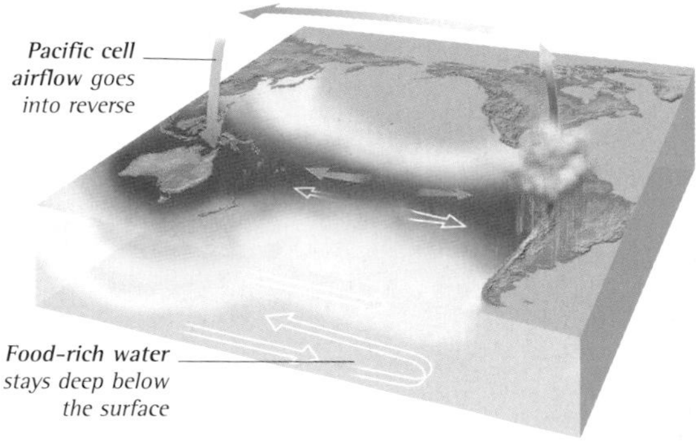

▲ EL NIÑO EVENT
In an El Niño event, the trade winds weaken, allowing warm surface water to flow back towards South America. The warm water prevents cold, food-rich water rising to the surface. This cuts off the food supply that supports the ocean wildlife. The extra warm surface water helps to create a low-pressure system over the eastern Pacific, causing heavy rain over South America and reversing the flow of the Pacific cell. Meanwhile, high pressure systems may form in the west, causing droughts.

Driving rain in Sydney during a La Niña event

◄ LA NIÑA
El Niño means "the little boy" in Spanish. It refers to the Christ Child, because the El Niño event often used to occur around Christmas. But sometimes the opposite happens, and the normal low-pressure system over the western Pacific becomes more intense. The trade winds strengthen, dragging warm water further west and improving the conditions for ocean life off South America. Low pressure in the west causes unusually heavy rain in Indonesia and Australia. This event is called La Niña, or "the little girl".

◄ EFFECT ON FISHING

The cold, plankton-rich waters off Peru are among the richest fishing grounds in the world. Vast numbers of fish are caught by commercial fishing boats like this one, hauling in its catch of anchovies. But a severe El Niño event stops the cold water coming to the surface, so there are no plankton and few fish. As a result, many people who depend on fishing lose their livelihood.

GLOBAL INFLUENCE ►

Because El Niño is linked to a change in air circulation that affects half the globe, its influence is felt far from the tropical Pacific. In 1992, atmospheric conditions related to an El Niño event produced three times the normal rainfall in Texas, freak storms in southern California, and temperatures that were up to 7°C (13°F) above normal in Alaska. They also caused a devastating drought in southern Africa that turned many fertile areas to desert.

THE NORTH ATLANTIC OSCILLATION

The Southern Oscillation is a regular event in the Pacific. Similar, but less extreme oscillations occur elsewhere. One is the North Atlantic Oscillation. This affects the pressure difference between two weather features, called the Azores High and the Iceland Low. When the difference between them is big, a strong polar jet stream carries wet and mild winter weather to northern Europe. But when the difference is small, the jet stream weakens, allowing cold air to move west, and bringing snowy winters to northern Europe.

▲ INDONESIAN DROUGHT

A normal year brings heavy rain to most parts of Indonesia and New Guinea. But the Southern Oscillation can create a high-pressure weather system over the region that prevents clouds and rain forming. The resulting drought can make crops die, causing widespread hardship. As the vegetation dries out, it catches fire easily, and large areas may be swept by destructive wildfires that the local farmers are not equipped to control.

DESERT RAIN ▼

In parts of Chile, high-pressure weather in normal years makes rainfall rare. This has helped to create the Atacama Desert (right) – the driest desert on Earth. During a severe El Niño event, the Southern Oscillation creates a low-pressure weather system over the Pacific coast of South America. This causes tropical rain and flooding, and occasionally makes the Atacama burst into bloom (below).

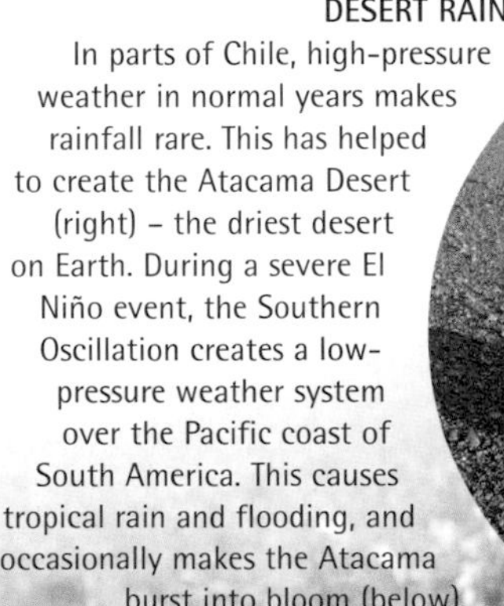

AIR POLLUTION AND SMOG

The air has always been affected by various forms of natural pollution, such as smoke from wildfires, or ash and gases from volcanic eruptions. These are part of the natural environment. But over the last 200 years, there has been a vast increase in artificial air pollution, caused by the growth of human populations, cities, and industry, and the use of cars and aircraft. At first this affected only cities and industrial regions, but now air pollution has spread all over the globe, and even affects the Arctic.

Aerosols are far too small to see without a microscope

AIRBORNE PARTICLES ►
The lower atmosphere contains countless tiny particles, called aerosols, which may stay suspended in the air for days. The particles shown here have been magnified by a scanning electron microscope. Some are natural materials such as dust, volcanic ash, fungus spores, and pollen grains. But others are soot and other substances emitted by vehicle engines and industry.

Coal smoke is full of suspended soot particles

◄ COAL SMOKE
Using coal as fuel can cause serious air pollution, because the smoke contains both polluting gases and soot particles. This mixture can blacken buildings, cause breathing difficulties, and stop plants growing properly. In the past, whole landscapes were blighted by coal smoke pollution, and it is still a major problem in some parts of the world.

ADAPTING TO POLLUTION

Smoke pollution was so widespread in 19th-century Britain that it affected the wildlife. The peppered moth usually has pale wings with dark speckling, but some individuals are much darker. In industrial regions, these darker moths were better camouflaged when they settled on smoke-blackened trees, and therefore less likely to be eaten by birds. As a result, the dark moth became more common than the pale one, but only in areas that suffered from serious air pollution.

ASH CLOUD ►
Volcanic eruptions are a natural occurrence, but their effects on the atmosphere can still be dramatic. In 1991, Mount Pinatubo in the Philippines erupted, blasting vast amounts of rock, fine ash, and gas up into the sky. The ash circled the Earth in a cloud that obscured the Sun and reduced average temperatures around the world by about 0.5°C (0.9°F).

▲ SMOG
Soot particles in the air help water vapour to condense easily (see page 40) and form fog. The result is a thick, poisonous, smoky fog, known as smog. Smog was common in cities such as London in Britain, seen here, when most homes were heated by coal fires. In December 1952, a severe London smog led to the deaths of up to 12,000 people, and as a result coal fires were banned in the city.

▲ PHOTOCHEMICAL SMOG
Car and truck engines produce gases that can react with ultraviolet light from the Sun to form a brown haze, called photochemical smog. This is common in sunny cities with lots of cars, such as Los Angeles in the USA. Here, the smog is made worse because a layer of cool oceanic air is often trapped beneath warmer air. This stops rising warm air carrying the pollutants away.

THE "YEAR WITHOUT A SUMMER"

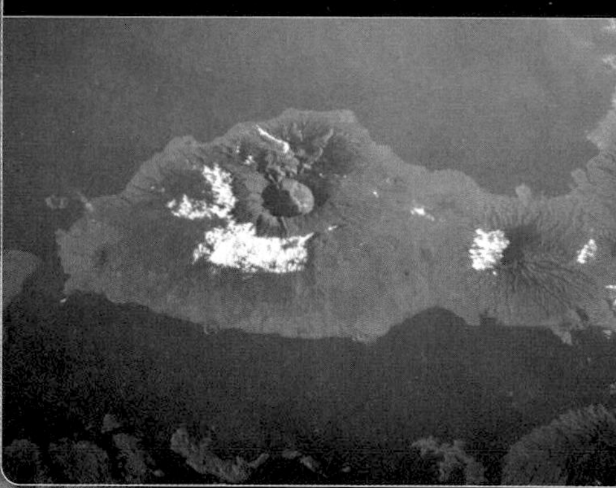

In 1815, the largest volcanic eruption ever recorded blew the top 1,200 m (4,000 ft) off Tambora, a volcano in Indonesia, seen here from space. Ash from Tambora circled the Earth and lowered world temperatures so much that 1816 became known as the "year without a summer". The cold summer weather stopped crops growing, causing food shortages and even famines. Grapes froze on the vines in France, and in Switzerland the starving people resorted to eating moss.

ASIATIC BROWN HAZE ►
In Asia, millions of cooking fires are producing a vast smoky cloud, known as the Asiatic brown haze. Air pollution caused by poisons in the smoke kills 2.2 million people a year, mainly women and children. Soot particles are carried around the world and even fall on Arctic ice, making it darker in colour. This makes the ice melt more easily (see page 17), so cooking fires in Asia may be helping to melt the polar ice sheets.

ACID RAIN AND OZONE DEPLETION

A lot of air pollution is caused by soot, ash, and other solid particles that form visible smoke clouds. But invisible gases, such as oxides of sulphur, nitrogen, and carbon, also pollute. All these occur naturally, but their concentration in the atmosphere has been increased by human activities. They are released by burning coal, oil, and gas in power plants, industry, vehicles, and homes, and cause pollution problems such as acid rain. Man-made gases called CFCs have also been released into the air, causing the destruction of atmospheric ozone.

▲ WASTE GASES
Acid rain is caused when water vapour dissolves oxides of sulphur and nitrogen from the air to form weak sulphuric and nitric acids. These acids then fall as rain. Most of the sulphur oxides are released by coal-burning power plants, while most of the nitric oxides come from petrol or diesel vehicles. Oxides can be filtered out of waste gases by devices such as catalytic converters in car exhausts, but these systems are not used everywhere and often do not work very efficiently.

DISSOLVING STONES

Many historic statues and buildings are made of limestone, a natural rock that is relatively easy to carve and shape into blocks. But limestone dissolves in acid. Since even natural rainwater is slightly acid, ancient stonework has suffered over the centuries, but the rate of decay has been greatly increased by air pollution. This gargoyle on Notre Dame Cathedral in Paris, France, has been partly eaten away by acid rain.

DEAD LAKES ►
In many regions, acid rain falls on lime-rich rocks, soils, and lakes. The lime reacts with the acid and makes it neutral, like pure water. But vast areas of Canada and Scandinavia are composed of hard, ancient rocks that do not contain any lime. Any acid rain that falls there makes the soil and lake waters increasingly acid, killing fish and other wildlife. Lake Erie in Canada, shown here, is just one of thousands of lakes affected in this way.

DYING TREES ►
In central and eastern Europe, Scandinavia, and Canada, millions of trees have been dying. This may be a result of acid rain damage, although some scientists believe that it is caused by photochemical smog (see page 77). Either way, the trees have been harmed by some form of air pollution, carried on the wind from big cities and industrial centres. Great tracts of forest have been destroyed, with catastrophic effects on the wildlife that lived there.

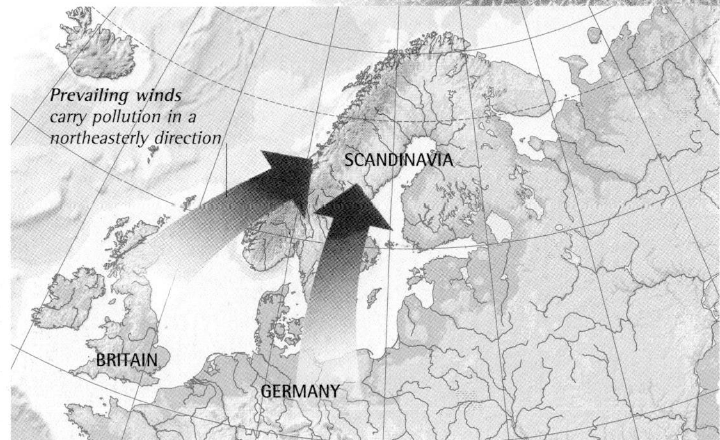

▲ DOWNWIND DESTRUCTION
The acidified water vapour that turns to acid rain is carried on the wind. So winds that blow over industrial areas and cities tend to carry the pollution to other regions. The countries of Scandinavia, for example, are badly affected by acid rain carried on the wind from Britain and north Germany, and this is a source of political tension in Europe. Canada has the same problem with pollution from the USA. But the situation is improving as pollution controls become more effective.

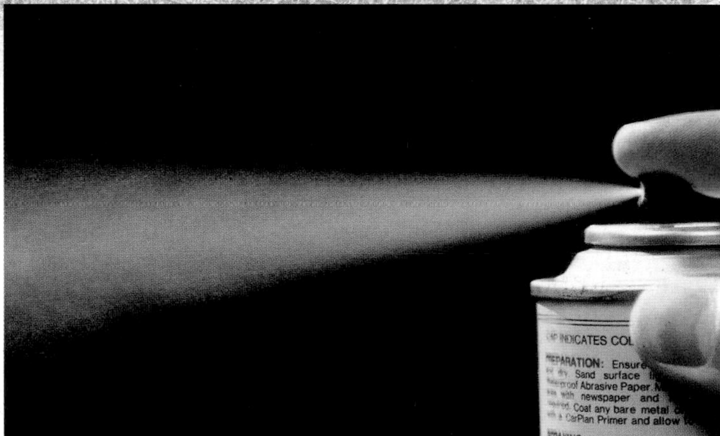

▲ OZONE DEPLETION
Ozone is a form of oxygen. There is a thin layer of ozone in the stratosphere, which absorbs dangerous ultraviolet (UV) radiation from the Sun (see page 16). Man-made gases called chlorofluorocarbons (CFCs) can destroy ozone. They were used for decades to pressurize aerosol cans, and are still used as the cooling agent in refrigerators. If CFCs are released into the atmosphere, they can attack and reduce the amount of ozone in the ozone layer.

FRIDGE MOUNTAIN

Once the effect of CFCs was known, steps were taken to limit their release. Can-makers switched to using "ozone-friendly" gases in aerosols, and systems have been set up to drain the CFCs safely from old refrigerators. But the CFCs already in the atmosphere decay very slowly, and will keep reacting with ozone for many decades. Meanwhile, the amount of CFCs released may increase again, as refrigeration becomes more widely used in the developing world.

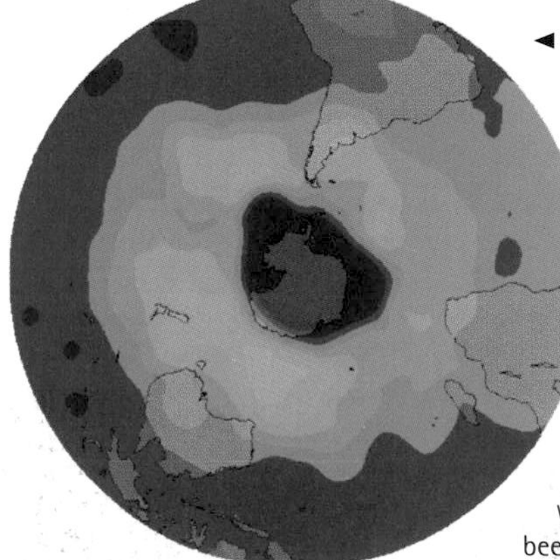

◄ OZONE HOLE
In 1983, scientists discovered a gap in the ozone layer, centred over the South Pole. In this satellite image, the hole is shown in dark blue. Temperatures below -78°C (-109°F) can help destroy ozone, so there is naturally less of it over Antarctica after the dark polar winter, but CFCs in the atmosphere may be making the problem worse. A smaller ozone hole has been detected over the Arctic.

CHANGING CLIMATES

Climates have been changing for as long as the Earth has existed. There are several reasons for this. Over time, the composition of the atmosphere has changed and the energy produced by the Sun has increased. Also, the continents are constantly moving, and this affects winds and ocean currents. The way the Earth orbits the Sun also varies according to predictable cycles. So over the millennia, most of the continents have experienced the whole range of climates, from tropical desert to frozen polar waste.

▲ THE EVOLVING ATMOSPHERE
About 3.6 billion years ago, there was far more carbon dioxide in the atmosphere than there is today. This caused a powerful greenhouse effect that, if it existed now, would make the oceans boil. But at the time, the Sun was producing 25 per cent less heat than it does today, so water was able to exist on Earth in its liquid form. The water gradually dissolved much of the carbon dioxide from the air and turned it into carbonate rocks, such as this limestone.

changing climates

◄ SHIFTING CONTINENTS
The huge plates that make up the Earth's crust are slowly moving, carrying the continents with them. The western Sahara, seen here, once lay at the South Pole, and was buried beneath ice. In contrast, parts of Antarctica were once covered by tropical forest. At times, the continents were joined together in giant super-continents, with central regions that lay so far from the ocean that it probably never rained there.

ORBITAL CYCLES

The Earth's orbit changes in regular cycles, and this affects the climate. These changes are called Milankovich cycles, after the Serbian climatologist Milutin Milankovich, who discovered them in 1920. There are three cycles, which all have different timescales. One affects the shape of the Earth's orbit round the Sun, which varies from a circular to an elliptical shape. Another cycle gradually alters the tilt of the Earth's axis relative to the Sun. The third cycle makes the tilted axis "wobble" or rotate. Together, they affect the global average temperature and seasonal extremes, as well as the timing of the seasons in different parts of the world. The cycles can also be linked to certain events in Earth's climate, such as some of the ice ages.

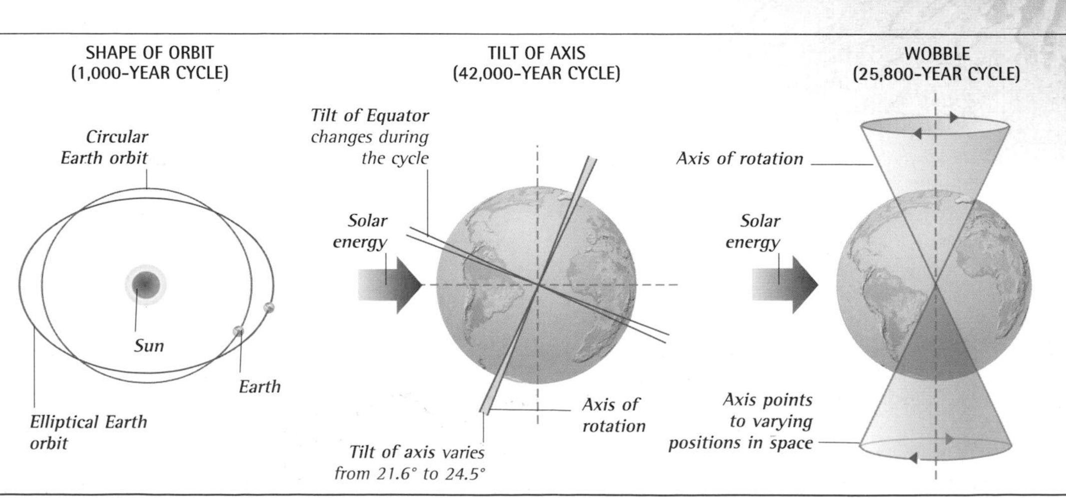

Arctic ice sheets were much bigger, and sea levels were lower 18,000 years ago

◄ ICE AGES
At various times in the Earth's history, the polar ice sheets have got bigger or smaller. The biggest fluctuations were probably caused by the changing positions of the continents. When the present pattern was established, about 2 million years ago, it led to an ice age that we still live in today. Just 18,000 years ago, the Arctic ice sheets covered Canada, Greenland, Scandinavia, northern Europe, and northern Russia.

WARM AND COLD PHASES

The most recent ice age has lasted for about 2 million years, but it has been interrupted by periods when the climate was frequently warmer than it is now. During the cold phases, much of the northern hemisphere resembled the Arctic (top). But 125,000 years ago, elephants and other tropical animals lived as far north as Britain. These warm and cold phases seem to have been caused by the Milankovich cycles. The last big freeze ended about 12,000 years ago, and we are currently living in a relatively warm phase. There will be more cold periods in the future, but not for at least 5,000 years.

THE LITTLE ICE AGE ►
On a smaller scale, climates often go through warm or cold periods that last for a few centuries. One of these was the "Little Ice Age" that began in about 1430 and lasted until roughly 1850. In Europe, the low temperatures allowed frost fairs to be held on the thick ice of frozen rivers and canals, as shown in this Dutch painting of about 1600.

Tyrannosaurus rex was one of the dinosaur species that died out 65 million years ago

▲ CATASTROPHES
Very occasionally, volcanic eruptions throw so much dust and gas into the atmosphere that they change the climate. Meteorite impacts like the one that created this crater in Australia can have the same effect. About 65 million years ago, an enormous meteorite crashed into Central America. Many experts believe that the colder weather this would have caused may have been responsible for the death of the dinosaurs. But a rival theory blames a series of big eruptions that occurred in India at the same time, releasing vast amounts of gas, and spilling molten rock over a huge area.

◄ MASS EXTINCTIONS
Most natural climate change occurs over such a long timescale that plants and animals are able to adapt to it, either by moving north and south, or by evolving to suit the new conditions. But some changes happen so quickly that the wildlife cannot cope with them, and simply dies out. Thousands of species were wiped out in the mass extinction that marked the end of the dinosaur era, about 65 million years ago.

GLOBAL WARMING

Research shows that the world is warming up. Since the 1880s, the global average temperature has risen by 1°C (1.8°F). That may not sound like much, but the world has warmed by less than 8°C (14.4°F) in the 12,000 years since the end of the last ice age. So an increase like this in one century is a lot. Rising temperatures are raising sea levels, melting polar ice, and upsetting the world's weather pattern. The problem is caused mainly by an increase in the greenhouse effect (see page 16), which people have brought about by burning fossil fuels.

global warming

CARBON CRISIS ▼

The increased greenhouse effect is mainly caused by extra carbon dioxide gas in the atmosphere. Recent research indicates that the level of carbon dioxide is higher now than it has been at any time in the last 625,000 years. Carbon dioxide is released by burning the coal, petrol, and other carbon-rich fuels that we use to power cars and aircraft and to generate the electricity that runs our homes.

***Each engine** may burn more than 3,000 litres (660 gallons) of fuel in just one hour*

MELTING ANTARCTIC ICE

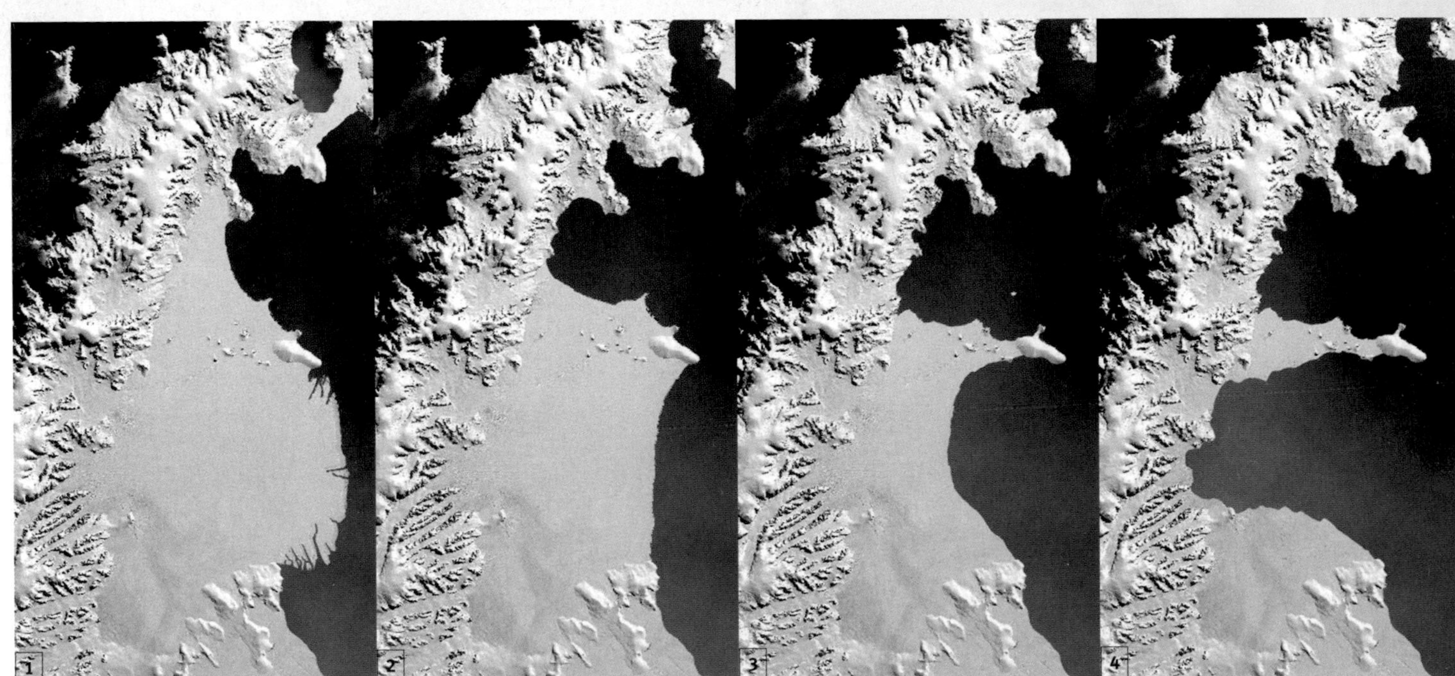

▲ 1993
Temperatures are rising fastest in the polar regions. On the Antarctic Peninsula, summers are 2°C (3.6°F) warmer than they were in the 1960s, and huge areas of ice have melted. This is the Larsen B ice shelf in 1993.

▲ 1995
The ice shelf once filled two very large bays, divided by a rocky headland. By 1995, half the ice in the northern bay had broken up, and a big area of ice on the outer edge of the southern section had also disappeared.

▲ 2000
Five years later, all the ice in the northern bay had gone. The ice sheet in the southern bay had also melted back, revealing a rocky headland that had been covered by thick, permanent ice for over 2,000 years.

▲ 2002
Within two years, another huge slab of ice had gone. In the nine years shown here, about 3,275 sq km (1,264 sq miles) of ice over 200 m (656 ft) thick had melted, or broken up into icebergs that drifted away into the Southern Ocean.

◄ ICE CORE EVIDENCE
An ice core is a sample of ice taken from deep inside an ice sheet. Ice cores from the Greenland and Antarctic ice sheets contain tiny air bubbles from the past 400,000 years. They show the proportions of gases in the atmosphere and indicate the air temperature at that time. Ice cores reveal that rising air temperatures coincide with higher levels of carbon dioxide. Scientists therefore believe that today's global warming is being caused by an increase in carbon dioxide.

VOLCANIC ERUPTIONS

Volcanoes can add vast amounts of carbon dioxide, water vapour, and other greenhouse gases to the atmosphere. A major eruption releases enough gas to make our human contribution seem small. But volcanoes have been erupting since the world began, so in the long term their effect on the atmosphere varies little. So volcanoes are not responsible for the current global warming.

Airliners release over 600 million tonnes of waste carbon dioxide each year

FOSSIL FUELS ►
Fossil fuels, such as coal, oil, and gas, are the remains of plants and animals that were fossilized many millions of years ago, complete with the carbon compounds that they contained. These carbon compounds store energy. When the fuels are burned, the energy is released, but the carbon is turned into carbon dioxide which then enters the atmosphere.

◄ BURNING FORESTS
Trees and other plants absorb carbon dioxide from the atmosphere when they are growing. They release it when they die and decay. So a natural forest, with young, old, and dead trees, absorbs as much carbon dioxide as it releases. But if the forest is cut down and burned, its entire carbon content is released into the atmosphere as carbon dioxide. This is happening throughout the tropics, where vast areas of forest are being destroyed each year.

METHANE ►
The natural gas that we use as fuel is a form of methane, a very powerful greenhouse gas. Although there is far less methane than carbon dioxide in the atmosphere, methane now causes about 20 per cent of the greenhouse effect. Methane is released from buried rubbish, rice paddy fields, and waterlogged swamps. It is increasing at an alarming rate, as frozen swamps in the Arctic thaw out and their dead vegetation starts to decay.

◄ GLOBAL DIMMING
The amount of energy from the Sun that reaches the Earth's surface has declined over the last 50 years, because of all the soot particles, urban smog, and other pollutants in the atmosphere. This is known as global dimming. It partly offsets the greenhouse effect, because there is less heat at ground level to be trapped by greenhouse gases. But if reducing air pollution also reduces the dimming effect, global warming could get worse in the future.

FUTURE CLIMATES

Predicting what climates will be like in the future is difficult. But most scientists agree that if global warming continues, it will do far more than make our weather warmer. It could create more deserts, destroy forests, flood coastal cities, and cause more extreme weather events. It may even disrupt ocean currents and melt polar ice sheets. As a result, many plants and animals could die out, and many people may suffer.

GLOBAL HEATWAVE

DROUGHT AND FAMINE
If temperatures continue to rise, there will be more droughts in continental regions. Existing deserts could grow, and regions that are now dry grassland or farmland might become deserts. The American prairies, for example, could easily become a barren dust bowl. Many people would have to abandon their homes, like these refugees fleeing from drought in Ethiopia, and many might starve.

SCORCHED EARTH
Droughts would cause more wildfires like this one, which destroyed 2,500 homes in California in 2003. Rainforests might not be able to survive the warmer conditions, and could burn too. If this happened, the burning would release even more carbon dioxide into the atmosphere. This would increase the greenhouse effect and accelerate global warming.

FLOODS AND STORMS

DROWNED CITIES
If oceans continue to warm up, more water will evaporate from them, more clouds will form, and more rain will fall over the land. Areas affected by oceanic weather systems, such as Europe, India, and southeast Asia, would suffer from more torrential rain. Rivers could overflow and flood cities, as happened in Prague in the Czech Republic in the summer of 2002.

HURRICANE WARNING
Warmer oceans would mean that hurricanes could form in regions that are further from the Equator. Experts believe that the storms may also get more severe, so catastrophes on the scale of Hurricane Katrina (see page 65) could become more frequent. The trend may have begun already, as the 2005 Atlantic hurricane season was the worst ever recorded.

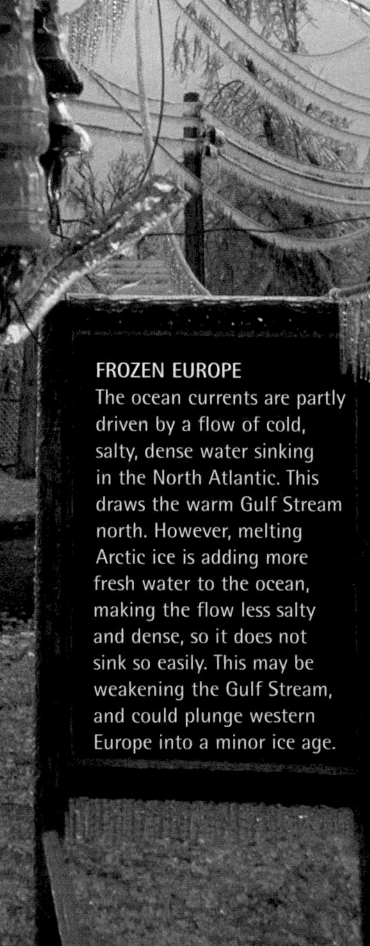

FROZEN EUROPE
The ocean currents are partly driven by a flow of cold, salty, dense water sinking in the North Atlantic. This draws the warm Gulf Stream north. However, melting Arctic ice is adding more fresh water to the ocean, making the flow less salty and dense, so it does not sink so easily. This may be weakening the Gulf Stream, and could plunge western Europe into a minor ice age.

future climates

▼ OCEAN THREAT
Warmer temperatures and melting ice are making sea levels rise. If this continues, low-lying islands such as the Maldives may disappear, and coastal cities like New York may be at risk. Wildlife is also under threat. As tropical oceans heat up, they dissolve more carbon dioxide, and become more acidic. This makes coral reefs die. Scientists now fear that the Great Barrier Reef may be dead by 2050.

▲ SHRINKING ICE SHEETS
The polar regions are warming up more quickly than any other part of the planet. Glaciers on the edges of the polar ice sheets have started flowing towards the sea much faster, melting, and adding to rising sea levels. The Arctic sea ice is only half as thick as it was 50 years ago, and its area is shrinking by 8 per cent each year. At the current rate of melting, the ice at the North Pole may completely disappear in 2060, and the polar bear could lose its habitat and become extinct.

CHECKS AND BALANCES ►
Some people believe that rising temperatures will trigger natural checks and balances that will keep the climate stable. For example, microscopic plankton in the oceans may multiply and combat the greenhouse effect by absorbing carbon dioxide. Also, more evaporation from warmer oceans would increase cloud cover, and this could have some cooling effect. However, the evidence indicates that temperatures are still rising, so while natural checks may slow global warming, they do not appear to be preventing it.

◄ RUNAWAY MELTDOWN
Other natural processes could make global warming worse. Large areas of Arctic permafrost are melting. If this continues, more tundra swamps like these will decay and release methane gas. This would enter the atmosphere and add to the greenhouse effect. The increase in water vapour rising off warmer oceans may have the same effect, because water vapour is a greenhouse gas. Also, as the reflective ice in the polar regions melts, the oceans and continents will absorb more of the Sun's energy, and heat up more quickly.

WEATHER MONITORING

Information about the weather is collected by weather stations all over the world and by orbiting satellites. The raw data is gathered by a wide variety of instruments. These range from simple devices, such as thermometers, wind vanes, and rain gauges, to the automatic sensors used to monitor the Earth's atmosphere from space. The data is put together to give an accurate picture of local or global weather at any one time, and is also used to make weather forecasts.

Cable is attached to a pack of instruments

▲ STEVENSON SCREEN
Many weather stations are collections of quite simple instruments. Their readings have to be recorded manually. This researcher is checking instruments at the Grenoble Snow Research Centre, in France. They are contained in a box called a Stevenson screen. This has white louvred sides which keep direct sunlight and wind off all the equipment inside. The instruments used for measuring wind, rain, and snowfall are mounted outside the box.

Halley Research Station in Antarctica

◄ WEATHER BALLOON
Helium-filled balloons are used to carry sensors high into the atmosphere. The sensors collect data on temperature, air pressure, humidity, and wind, and transmit this back to a base station by radio. Each balloon expands as it rises owing to the reduced air pressure around it, and eventually bursts. The instrument pack, or radiosonde, then falls back to the ground by parachute and, if possible, is recovered.

BASIC INSTRUMENTS

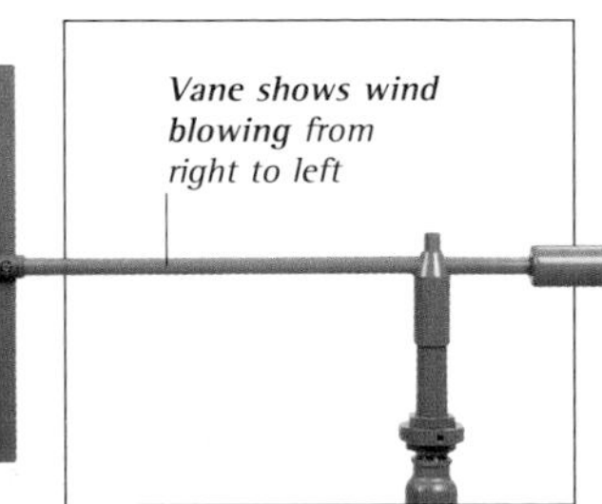

Vane shows wind blowing from right to left

WIND VANE
This instrument, called a wind vane, shows wind direction. It swivels round to point in the direction the wind is blowing. A basic wind vane can be read by eye. This one is linked to an electronic sensor, which displays the wind direction as a compass bearing. This data can also be transmitted by radio, or fed into a computer.

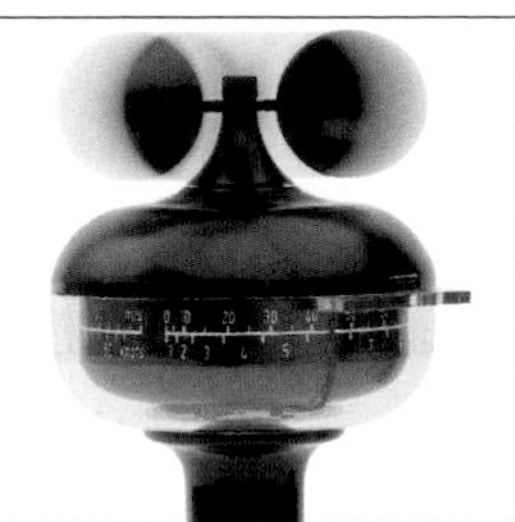

ANEMOMETER
Wind speed is measured by an instrument called an anemometer. The faster the wind blows, the faster it spins round. This hand-held model gives a wind speed reading on a scale. Others are electronically connected to base stations, so the wind speed is recorded automatically.

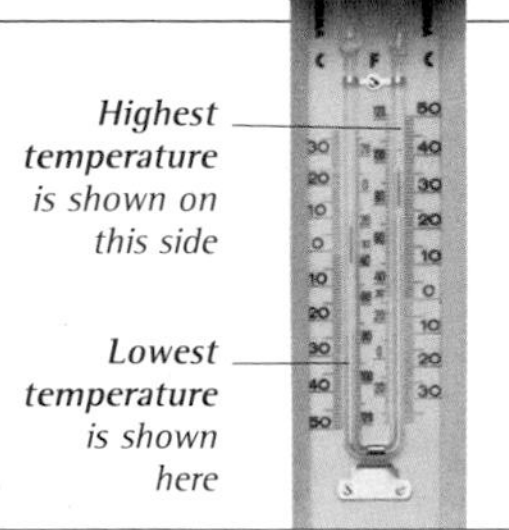

Highest temperature is shown on this side

Lowest temperature is shown here

THERMOMETER
A thermometer measures temperature. This U-shaped thermometer shows the current temperature, and also records the maximum and minimum temperatures since it was last checked. It needs to be read manually, but other types of thermometer are linked to radio transmitters and computers.

RAIN GAUGE
A rain gauge measures how much rain has fallen. It consists of a collecting jar placed in a metal container. At the top of the container is a funnel that collects the rain over a known area. The water in the jar is poured into a glass measuring cylinder to determine how much rain has fallen. There are also electronic versions.

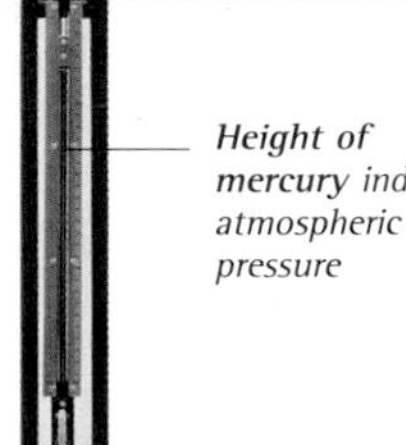

Height of mercury indicates atmospheric pressure

BAROMETER
A barometer measures atmospheric pressure. Simple aneroid barometers give a reading on a dial, or through an electronic link, but mercury barometers like this one are more accurate. Air pressure forces the heavy mercury up the tube.

AUTOMATIC ARRAY ►
Thousands of automatic weather stations are used to gather weather data worldwide. Each weather station consists of an array of weather instruments, electronically linked to a radio transmitter. Several times a day, the data it collects is automatically sent to weather centres all over the world through satellite links.

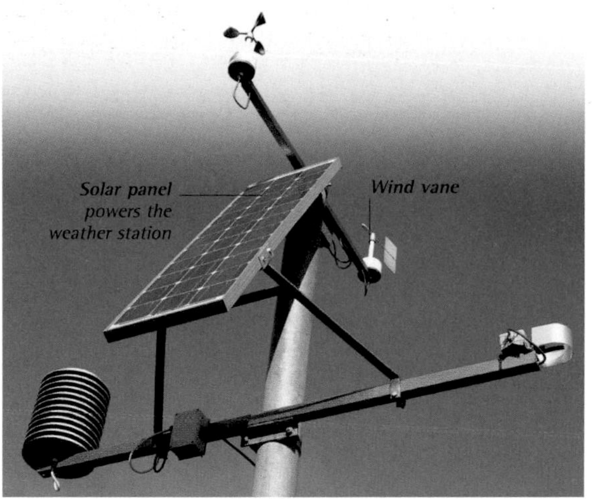

Anemometers measure wind speed

Fin ensures that the buoy always points in the same direction as the wind

WEATHER BUOY ►
Gathering weather data at sea is extremely important. Ships' crews rely on accurate marine weather forecasts, and the data also helps to predict the weather on land. Some information is obtained from commercial ships, but there are also special weather ships and weather buoys like this one. A buoy is a floating, automatic weather station, which is either anchored or allowed to drift with the ocean currents.

Weather satellites are carried into space on unmanned rockets

Satellite is packed with *instruments* to gather weather data

▲ WEATHER SATELLITE
Satellites launched into space by rockets provide valuable weather data. This is a geostationary satellite, which orbits the Earth above the Equator at a height of 36,000 km (22,500 miles). At this altitude, it remains above one place on the ground. It uses special sensors to monitor temperature, clouds, wind, and humidity, and transmits the information back to Earth.

SENSING THE WEATHER

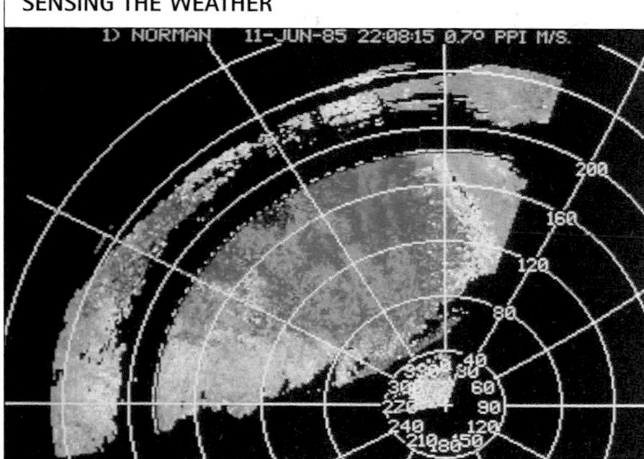

As well as satellites, there are numerous other methods for measuring the weather remotely. Radar equipment can be used to detect rainfall, for example. A pulse of radio waves is transmitted through the atmosphere. The amount of reflection and the time it takes to occur allow meteorologists to measure the rate of rainfall over a wide area. This Doppler radar image shows wind speeds during a squall over Oklahoma, USA. Scans like this one can be used to detect tornadoes.

▼ WEATHER PLANE
Weather planes cruise the sky taking measurements and samples. They are expensive to run, so there are not many of them, but many commercial aeroplanes now also make routine weather observations. This weather plane is operated by the US government. It flies into hurricanes to gather information on wind speeds, air pressure, and humidity.

Sensors mounted on stalks probe the atmosphere

Pilots are trained to fly right through hurricanes

◄ WEATHER CHECK
National weather centres produce regular weather reports, usually twice a day. They are sent to weather forecasters, who convert them into formats that are easy to understand. These range from basic weather checks on the radio, to detailed weather maps and data that are transmitted to people such as sailors. Displayed on screen, these maps enable users to understand the weather situation, and forecast the weather for their own area.

__Sailors__ depend on accurate weather forecasts

WEATHER FORECASTING

Meteorologists use the data from weather stations to work out what the weather will do next. Often the data fits a recognized pattern, such as a low-pressure system, so they can predict the general outcome easily. But forecasting the weather in detail is more difficult. It is particularly hard to say where local events such as hailstorms may strike. Computers have made forecasts more accurate, but a lot still depends on the skill of the forecaster.

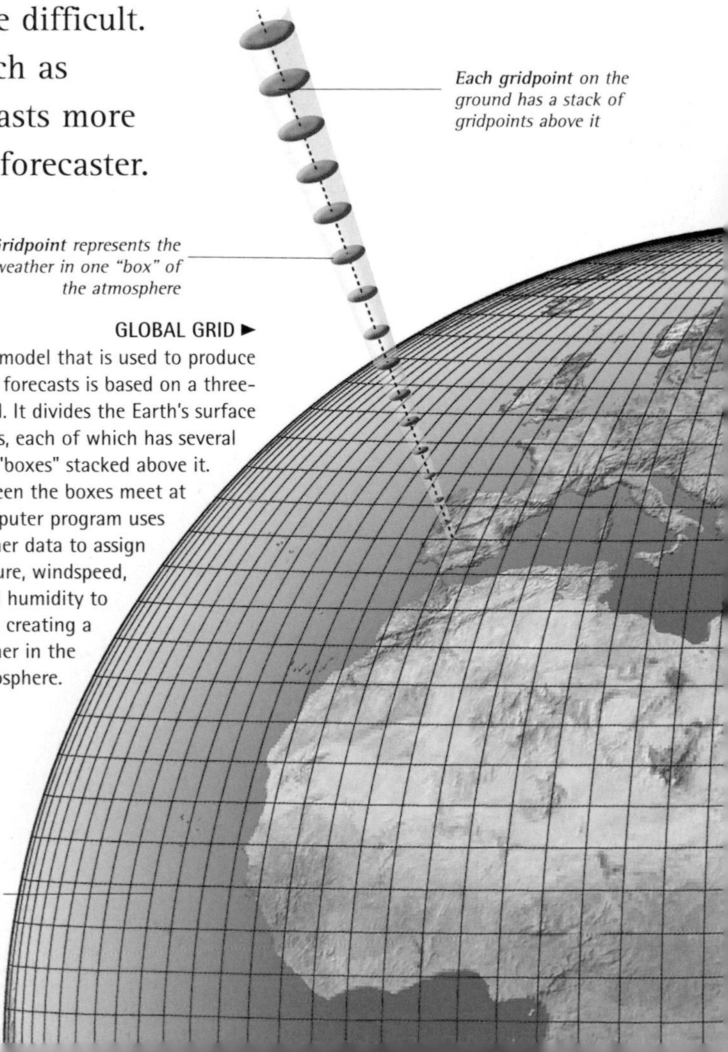

__Each gridpoint__ on the ground has a stack of gridpoints above it

__Gridpoint__ represents the weather in one "box" of the atmosphere

__Computer imagery__ helps meteorologists to interpret raw data

▲ COMPUTER PROGRAM
Nearly all weather forecasting now relies on computers. Information gathered from hundreds of weather monitoring stations and satellites is entered into a special computer program, which is a mathematical model of the moving atmosphere. When this program is run, it uses the latest weather observations to produce a set of numbers that shows how the state of the atmosphere is likely to change. Meteorologists can then turn this information into a weather forecast.

GLOBAL GRID ►
The computer model that is used to produce weather forecasts is based on a three-dimensional grid. It divides the Earth's surface into squares, each of which has several imaginary "boxes" stacked above it. The lines between the boxes meet at gridpoints. The computer program uses the latest weather data to assign values of temperature, windspeed, pressure, and humidity to each gridpoint, creating a map of the weather in the atmosphere.

__Grid lines__ divide the Earth's surface into squares

WEATHER MAPS ►
Newspaper weather forecasts are often given in the form of maps. Some maps show how weather systems are moving and give data such as atmospheric pressure and weather fronts, as in this circular map. The black lines, or isobars, mark two centres of low pressure over northern and south-eastern Europe. Other maps have symbols indicating the type of weather to be expected, such as sunny spells, light rain, or strong winds. A map of this type is shown on the far right.

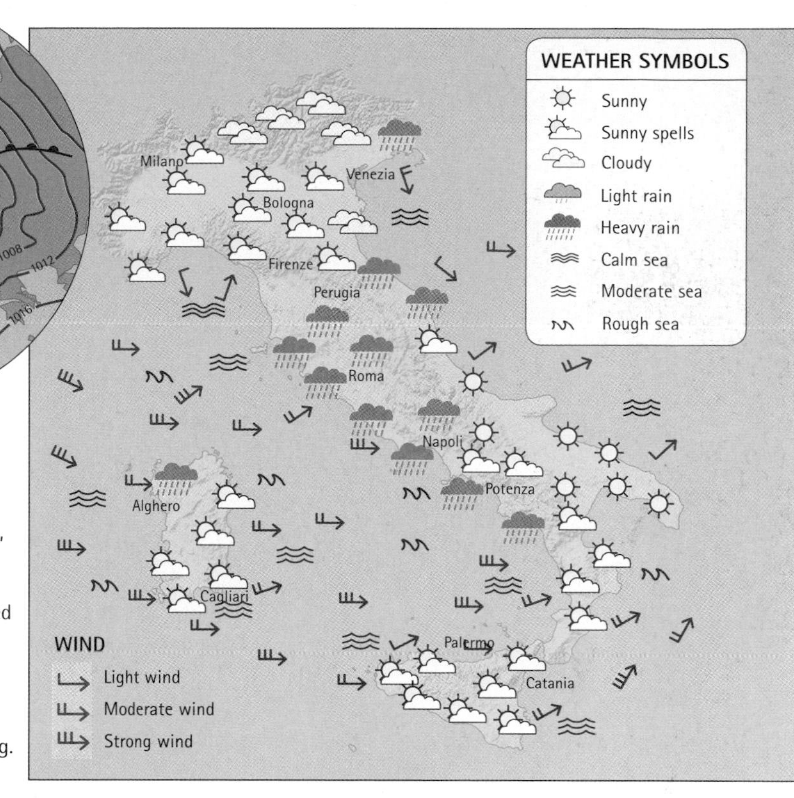

◄ WEATHER ON TV
On a TV weather forecast, the forecaster is in fact standing in front of a blank blue screen, pointing at nothing. In the finished broadcast, the blue areas are electronically replaced by maps and other effects. These images also appear on a small TV monitor next to the blue screen, so the forecaster can see what he or she is doing. Getting it right takes practice.

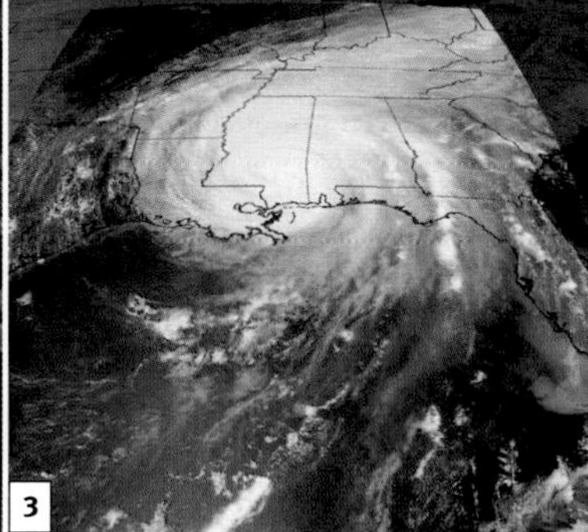

◄ SATELLITE IMAGES
If you visit the websites of national weather centres, you can view images transmitted by weather satellites. These include pictures of the current weather over various parts of the world, and sequences that show the progress of major weather systems. This three-part sequence shows Hurricane Katrina as it moved over New Orleans in the southern USA, in August 2005.

WATCHING THE WEATHER ►
Everyone is interested in the weather forecast, but some people rely on it. A farmer may need to wait while a crop ripens in the sun, then harvest it quickly before it is flattened by a rainstorm. For him, an accurate weather forecast can make the difference between profit and loss. Pilots, airport controllers, coastguards, and fishing boat skippers are just a few of the many people whose work and safety depends on good weather forecasting.

Farmers rely on weather forecasts to warn them about approaching storms

KEY EVENTS AND DISCOVERIES

c.200 BC The Greek inventor, Hero of Alexandria, discovers that air has weight.

AD 23 Greek geographer Strabo publishes his *Geographical Sketches*, which include the observation that the Earth has cold, temperate, and tropical climate zones.

1430 Europe enters the "Little Ice Age" that lasts until the 19th century. The low temperatures make rivers and canals freeze each winter, and cause widespread crop failures and famines.

1492 On his voyage to the Caribbean, Christopher Columbus becomes the first European to use the trade winds to cross the Atlantic Ocean from east to west.

1564 Thanks to the cold weather of the Little Ice Age, the first Frost Fair is held on the frozen River Thames in London, UK. Tents, sideshows, and food stalls are erected on the thick ice.

1611 German astronomer Johannes Kepler is the first person to describe the six-sided shape of snowflakes.

1644 Italian physicist Evangelista Torricelli invents the mercury barometer, for measuring atmospheric pressure.

1654 Grand Duke Ferdinand of Tuscany, Italy invents the first sealed thermometer for measuring temperature. He also invents the condensation hygrometer for measuring humidity.

1662 British architect and scientist Christopher Wren invents the first modern rain gauge.

1679 British astronomer Edmund Halley links air pressure with altitude and recognizes that the warmth of the Sun creates currents in the atmosphere.

1687 British scientist Isaac Newton publishes the *Mathematical Principles of Natural Philosophy,* known as the *Principia*, which explains the basic laws of motion.

1703 Britain's most severe storm on record, known as the "Great Storm", destroys many towns and kills 123 people on land. Another 8,000 people are thought to have drowned at sea.

1718 German scientist Gabriel Daniel Fahrenheit devises the Fahrenheit scale (°F) for measuring temperature.

1735 British physicist George Hadley explains how the Earth's rotation affects the trade winds. His name is given to the Hadley Cells, which are part of the pattern of global air circulation.

1742 Swedish scientist Anders Celsius devises the Celsius (Centigrade) scale (°C) for measuring temperature.

1752 American scientist and statesman Benjamin Franklin uses a kite to investigate lightning – an experiment that leads to his invention of the lightning conductor.

1803 British amateur meteorologist Luke Howard publishes the first of his *Notes on the Modifications of the Clouds*, in which he develops the system for naming clouds that is still used today.

1805 British Admiral Francis Beaufort devises a scale for measuring wind speed at sea. It is later modified for use on land too.

1815 The largest volcanic eruption in recorded history causes the explosion of the Indonesian volcano, Tambora. Airborne ash circling the Earth results in the "year without a summer" of 1816.

1827 French mathematician Jean Baptiste Fourier discovers the greenhouse effect, by which the atmosphere traps heat that is radiated from the Sun-warmed Earth.

1835 French physicist Gustave-Gaspard de Coriolis publishes a paper describing the way air and water move over the spinning Earth. This becomes known as the Coriolis effect.

1840 Swiss-born scientist Louis Agassiz proposes his theory of ice ages, and suggests that northern Europe was once covered by an ice sheet.

1848 Joseph Henry of the Smithsonian Institution sets up a system for obtaining weather reports from across the USA. Soon, 200 observers are sending weather data to Henry, enabling him to provide daily weather reports for the *Washington Evening Post.*

1856 US teacher William Ferrel discovers that mid-latitude circulation cells exist between the Polar and Hadley cells. These are known as Ferrel cells.

1857 Dutch meteorologist Christoph Buys Ballot explains how centres of high and low atmospheric pressure influence wind speed and direction.

1863 Irish scientist John Tyndall publishes a paper describing how water vapour can act as a greenhouse gas.

1892 The first weather balloons are flown in France. They carry instruments that record atmospheric pressure, temperature, and humidity in the atmosphere.

1895 Swedish chemist Svante Arrhenius suggests that adding carbon dioxide to the Earth's atmosphere by burning fossil fuels might increase the greenhouse effect and cause global warming.

1899 Australia suffers the most deadly cyclone-related disaster in its history, when more than 300 people are killed in the "Bathurst Bay Hurricane".

1900 The town of Galveston in Texas, USA is destroyed by a hurricane. The storm surge and resulting floods kill more than 8,000 people.

1912 On 15 April, the *Titanic* is sunk by a collision with an iceberg that has drifted 700 km (435 miles) southeast of Newfoundland, Canada. 1,500 people die.

1913 One of the most severe storms ever recorded in Canada – the Black Sunday Storm – sweeps over Lake Erie and Lake Ontario, sinking 34 ships and drowning 270 sailors.

1916 The Clermont region of northeastern Australia is hit by catastrophic flooding during a La Niña year, when rainfall in the western Pacific region is unusually high.

1920 Serbian scientist Milutin Milankovitch discovers how variations in the Earth's orbit around the Sun cause cycles of fluctuating global temperature.

1921 Norwegian meteorologist Vilhelm Bjerknes publishes a major study of the atmosphere, identifying air masses and fronts. This forms the basis of modern weather forecasting.

1922 British physicist Lewis Richardson uses mathematical calulations to forecast the weather. However, this method does not become practical until the invention of computers.

1922 The world's highest ever temperature – 58°C (136°F) – is recorded at Al Aziziyah in Libya.

1925 The most deadly American tornado on record, the Tri-State Twister, leaves a trail of destruction through the states of Missouri, Illinois, and Indiana in the USA, killing 695 people.

1931 The Yangtze River in China floods, causing the death of 3.7 million people through disease, starvation, or drowning. This flood is the most destructive weather event in recorded history.

1932 After years of drought and overcropping, the soil of the American Midwest has been reduced to dust and starts to blow away. These dust storms continue until 1939.

1934 A "coldwave" grips eastern North America, from Canada to Florida. Lake Ontario freezes over completely for only the second time in recorded history.

1936 A heatwave strikes the provinces of Manitoba and Ontario, in Canada. Temperatures exceed 44°C (111°F) for several days and 1,180 people die. The heat is so intense that steel railway lines and bridge girders twist, and fruit is baked on the trees.

1939 In southern Australia, a heatwave kills 438 people and the "Black Friday" fires destroy many towns around Melbourne.

1940 Jim Fidler presents the first ever television weather forecast, for an experimental station in Cincinnati, USA.

1945 High-flying US military pilots discover the jet streams – bands of fast-moving air that blow around the world at high altitude, just below the stratosphere.

1947 The coldest ever temperature in North America is recorded on 3 February, when the the temperature in Snag, Yukon Territories, Canada dips to –63°C (–81°F).

1948 US oceanographer Henry Melson Stommel publishes a paper explaining the workings of the Gulf Stream and the ocean circulation that redistributes heat around the world.

1950 One of the first electronic computers, called ENIAC (Electronic Numerical Integrator and Computer), produces the world's first ever computerized weather forecast.

1952 In London, UK, a severe smog leads to the deaths of up to 12,000 people. As a result, coal fires are banned in the city.

1953 Storms in the North Sea combine with high tides to flood low-lying parts of eastern England and the Netherlands. More than 2,000 people die.

1957 US oceanographer Roger Revelle warns that humanity is conducting a "large-scale geophysical experiment" on the planet by releasing greenhouse gases.

1960 The world's first weather satellite is launched from Cape Canaveral in Florida, USA. It is called the Television Infrared Observation Satellite, or TIROS.

1962–63 Britain suffers its coldest winter on record since 1740, with an average temperature of only 0.8°C (33.4°F).

1966 The world's heaviest rainfall is recorded at Foc-Foc on the island of Réunion in the Indian Ocean. In just one day, 182.5 cm (72 in) of rain falls.

1970 The worst tropical storm of the 20th century occurs in Bangladesh. High winds and flooding caused by the storm surge kill 300,000–500,000 people.

1971 Japanese-American meteorologist T. Theodore Fujita devises a six-category scale to classify tornadoes. In the same year, Robert Simpson and Herbert Saffir come up with the Saffir-Simpson Scale for measuring the strength of hurricanes.

1974 The town of Darwin in northern Australia is virtually destroyed by tropical cyclone Tracy.

1980 US scientists Luis and Walter Alvarez claim that a meteorite impact 65 million years ago on what is now the Yucatán Peninsula in Mexico, could have caused the sudden change in world climates that wiped out the dinosaurs.

1982 Swiss physicist Hans Oeschger, working on atmospheric samples trapped in the Greenland ice, discovers the link between levels of carbon dioxide gas in the atmosphere and global warming.

1982–83 An El Niño event disrupts the weather throughout the Pacific region. Stocks of fish off Ecuador and Peru in the Eastern Pacific are virtually destroyed.

1983 The world's lowest ever temperature is recorded at Vostok Base in Antarctica, when the temperature drops to –89.2°C (–128.6°F).

1985 During spring in Antarctica, scientists from the British Antarctic Survey record a hole in the ozone layer over the continent.

1987 The most violent storm recorded since 1703 sweeps through southern Britain, uprooting more than 15 million trees.

1990 US geophysicist Syukuro Manabe uses a computer model of the world's climate to show that global warming could shut down the Gulf Stream, making northern Europe colder rather than warmer.

1991 Mount Pinatubo in the Philippines erupts, spilling a dust cloud into the atmosphere that causes temporary global cooling. Average temperatures around the world drop for two years before rising again.

1991–92 Africa suffers its worst dry spell of the 20th century when an area of 6.7 million sq km (2.6 million sq miles) is affected by drought.

1995 During hurricane Luis, the largest ocean wave ever recorded strikes the *QE2* liner off the coast of Newfoundland, Canada. The wave is 30 m (98 ft) high.

1998 Hurricane Mitch strikes Central America, causing huge damage and killing more than 11,000 people.

1998 Canada suffers the "Ice Storm of the Century", which destroys millions of trees and brings down 120,000 km (75,000 miles) of power and telephone lines.

2003 Europe experiences its hottest summer for at least 500 years, causing about 30,000 deaths.

2004 Measurements of ocean currents associated with the Gulf Stream show that the flow has slowed by 30 per cent since the 1960s. They suggest that the Gulf Stream may be under serious threat.

2005 The British Antarctic Survey reveals that the massive West Antarctic ice sheet could be disintegrating – an event which would raise world sea levels by up to 5 m (16 ft), flooding low-lying coastal regions and cities.

2005 Hurricane Katrina destroys the city of New Orleans in the southern USA, causing the deaths of more than 1,000 people. The year 2005 is the worst Atlantic hurricane season on record, with 27 named storms, of which 14 are hurricanes.

GLOSSARY

Air mass A large body of air, that is warm or cold, and wet or dry, depending on where it has come from.

Albedo The percentage of the Sun's energy that is reflected by a surface. A reflective surface, like ice, has a high albedo of about 80 per cent.

Altitude Height above sea level.

Anticyclone An area of high atmospheric pressure, in which cool air is sinking, then spreading out at ground or sea level.

Arctic Circle An imaginary line around the Earth, at latitude 66°34'N. The Arctic Circle marks the limit of the region that experiences 24-hour sunlight in midsummer.

Arid Very dry, as in a desert.

Atmosphere The layer or layers of gas that surround a planet, such as Earth.

Atmospheric pressure The pressure created by the weight of air in the atmosphere pressing down on the Earth's surface. It is normally measured at sea level.

Axis An imaginary line around which something rotates.

Carbon dioxide A gas that forms a very small percentage of the atmosphere. Living things such as plants use carbon dioxide to make food, and it is also a greenhouse gas.

Climate The typical, or average, weather in a particular area.

Cloud base The lowest part of a cloud.

Coalescence The process by which two water droplets merge into one.

Condensation nuclei Tiny airborne particles that attract water vapour and allow it to condense into droplets of liquid water.

Condense To turn from a gas to a liquid.

Continental climate A type of climate with cold winters and hot, dry summers that is typical of regions in the middle of large landmasses.

Convection The movement and circulation of gases and liquids in response to heat.

Convection cell Gas or liquid that is circulating round and round, powered by heat.

Convection clouds Clouds formed when moist air is warmed and rises.

Coriolis effect The way the Earth's spin affects objects, or masses of air or water, that are moving across its surface.

Current A flow of air or water.

Cyclone An area of low atmospheric pressure, in which warm air is being sucked in and rising. A cyclone is also known as a depression, or low.

Density The compactness of a substance. If a substance is squeezed together, it becomes more dense.

Depression An area of low atmospheric pressure, in which warm air is being sucked in and rising. It is also known as a cyclone, or low.

Downdraught A current of air that flows downwards.

Dust bowl An artificial desert caused by a combination of drought and growing too many crops on dry soil, so the soil turns to dust.

Electromagnetic spectrum The entire range of energy radiated by the Sun, from very short-wave gamma-rays to very long-wave radio waves, and including visible light.

Equator An imaginary line around the middle of the Earth at its broadest point.

Evaporate To turn from a liquid to a gas.

Eye The calm centre of a tropical revolving storm, or hurricane.

Ferrel cell A large-scale air circulation system, in which air sinks near the tropics, flows towards a polar region and then rises at a polar front.

Flash flood A flood that rises very quickly after a heavy rainstorm, and may form a powerful torrent of water.

Front The leading edge of a moving air mass. If the air mass is warm, its leading edge is called a warm front. The leading edge of a cold air mass is called a cold front.

Glacier A mass of ice that flows very slowly downhill, like a frozen river.

Gravity The force of attraction exerted by a large object, such as a planet. Gravity holds things on the planet's surface.

Greenhouse effect The warming effect caused by the way atmospheric gases, such as carbon dioxide, methane, and water vapour, absorb some of the heat radiated from the Earth.

Hadley cell A large-scale air circulation system, in which air rises near the Equator, flows away to the north or south, sinks near the Tropic of Cancer or Capricorn, and then flows back towards the Equator.

Haze A misty effect caused by microscopic dust or smoke particles suspended in the air.

High A high-pressure weather system, also known as an anticyclone.

Humidity The amount of water vapour in the air.

Hurricane A very destructive revolving storm that may develop from a tropical depression. Also known as a tropical cyclone, or a typhoon.

Infrared Long-wave energy that is invisible, but is felt as heat. Its wavelength is just longer than that of red light.

Intertropical convergence zone (ITCZ) The area near the Equator where warm, moist air is rising. The ITCZ moves north and south with the seasons, and is marked by deep clouds.

Isobar A line on a weather map linking places that have the same atmospheric pressure.

Jet stream A relatively strong wind, concentrated in a narrow stream, that blows round the world at high altitude.

Landmass A large area of land, such as a continent.

Latent heat Energy in the form of heat that is absorbed or released when a material undergoes a change of state. For example, latent heat is released when a material changes from a gas to a liquid.

Latitude The location of a place north or south of the Equator. Latitude is measured in degrees, with 90° at the poles and 0° at the Equator.

Low A low-pressure weather system, also known as a depression, or cyclone.

Maritime climate A climate that is strongly influenced by a nearby ocean. It has cool summers, mild winters, and regular rain.

Mass The amount of matter out of which a body is composed. Mass is also used to describe a large volume of something, such as air.

Mesopause The boundary between the mesosphere and the thermosphere, two layers of the Earth's atmosphere.

Mesosphere The layer of Earth's atmosphere that lies above the stratosphere.

Meteorologist A scientist who studies the weather.

Meteors Fragments of rock that fall from space into Earth's atmosphere. Meteors are heated by friction, so they burn up as "shooting stars". Meteors that reach the Earth's surface are called meteorites.

Mid-latitudes The regions that lie between the warm subtropics and the cold polar regions.

Millibar A unit used to measure atmospheric pressure. The world's average sea level atmospheric pressure is 1013 millibars (mb).

Molecule The smallest amount of a chemical substance that can exist. It is made of atoms of the elements that make up that substance. A water molecule, for example, consists of two hydrogen atoms and one oxygen atom.

Monsoon A seasonal change of wind that affects the weather, especially in the Indian subcontinent and other tropical regions, where it causes wet and dry seasons.

Native Naturally found in a particular place, and not introduced by people.

Northern hemisphere The northern half of the Earth, lying north of the Equator.

Nuclear fusion The process by which the cores, or nuclei, of small atoms fuse together to form larger, heavier nuclei, releasing large amounts of energy.

Nucleus The central mass of something, such as an atom, or the object around which something like a water droplet grows. The plural of nucleus is nuclei.

Occlusion The final phase in the life of a depression, when a moving cold front catches up with a warm front and lifts the warm air mass off the ground. The warm and cold fronts then combine to form an occluded front.

Orbit To travel round a star, planet, or moon. Earth orbits the Sun, and satellites orbit Earth.

Orographic cloud Cloud formed in air that is forced to rise over high ground.

Oxygen A gas that makes up one-fifth of the Earth's atmosphere at sea level. Oxygen is vital to all living things, which use it to turn food into energy.

Ozone A gas that is formed from oxygen. It can occur at ground level, but also forms a layer in the atmosphere that absorbs some of the ultraviolet radiation in sunlight.

Permafrost Frozen ground that never thaws out.

Polar Associated with the North Pole or South Pole, or the regions around them.

Polar cell A large-scale air circulation system, in which air sinks near the North Pole or South Pole, flows towards the tropics, and then rises at a Polar front.

Polar easterlies Prevailing winds that blow from the east in the regions near the North or South Poles.

Polar front A large-scale boundary between air masses. At the polar front, cold air that is moving away from the polar regions pushes underneath warmer air that is moving away from the tropics.

Pollution Anything harmful added to the natural environment, usually by people, that is not part of its normal make-up.

Precipitation Water that falls from clouds to the ground in the form of rain, hail, or snow.

Pressure gradient The difference between areas of high and low atmospheric pressure. Air flows from a high-pressure zone to a low-pressure zone as wind. The steeper the pressure gradient, the stronger the wind.

Prevailing wind The wind that normally blows in a particular area at a particular time.

Radiate To emit electromagnetic rays or waves through an atmosphere or space. Visible light and heat from the Sun are forms of radiation.

Rain shadow The result of the moisture in the air falling as rain on one side of a mountain ridge, so there is none left to fall on the other side. The dry side is in the rain shadow.

Seasonal wind A wind that blows only during certain seasons of the year.

Smog A form of air pollution, usually caused by smoke particles attracting water vapour to form a smoky fog.

Solar To do with the Sun.

Solar System The system of planets, moons, and asteroids orbiting the Sun.

Southern hemisphere The southern half of the Earth, lying south of the Equator.

Stratopause The boundary between the stratosphere and the mesosphere, two layers of the Earth's atmosphere.

Stratosphere The layer of Earth's atmosphere that lies above the troposphere.

Subtropics The warm regions to the north and south of the Equator that lie between the hot tropics and the cooler mid-latitudes.

Supercooled Cooled to below the temperature at which a substance normally turns into a different state. This often describes water that has been cooled to below freezing point without turning to ice.

Temperature inversion A situation where the normal drop in temperature with altitude is reduced or reversed. For example, higher altitude air is usually cooler than lower altitude air, but in a temperature inversion the higher level air is warmer.

Thermal To do with heat.

Thermal inertia Slowness to gain or lose heat. Ocean water has high thermal inertia, so it loses and gains heat more slowly than the land.

Thermosphere The outermost layer of the Earth's atmosphere.

Tornado A violent, very concentrated revolving storm, caused by air swirling into a small region of extremely low atmospheric pressure.

Trade wind A wind that blows steadily from east to west over a tropical ocean. Trade winds north of the Equator blow from the northeast; southern trade winds blow from the southeast.

Tropic of Cancer An imaginary line around the Earth, marking the point where the Sun shines directly overhead on 21 June. It is the northern limit of the tropics.

Tropic of Capricorn An imaginary line around the Earth, marking the point where the Sun shines directly overhead on 21 December. It is the southern limit of the tropics.

Tropics The hot regions to the north and south of the Equator, which lie between the Tropic of Cancer and the Tropic of Capricorn.

Tropopause The boundary between the troposphere – the lowest layer of the atmosphere – and the stratosphere above.

Troposphere The layer of the Earth's atmosphere that is closest to the surface and contains our weather.

Tundra The cold, treeless landscape that lies on the edges of the polar ice sheets.

Turbulence Irregular, often violent, currents of moving air or water.

Ultraviolet (UV) Short-wave energy radiated by the Sun. UV is invisible, but causes sunburn and skin cancer. Its wavelength is just shorter than that of violet light.

Upcurrent or **updraught** An air or water current that flows upwards.

Visible spectrum The part of the electromagnetic spectrum that contains visible light. It includes all the colours of the rainbow, from red to violet, which if added together form white sunlight.

Vortex A spiralling movement, where air or water is being drawn into the centre and then up or down, like water going down a plughole.

Water vapour The invisible gas formed when liquid water is warmed and evaporates.

Wave clouds Clouds that develop at the cool crests of waves in a flow of air. The waves are usually created when air rises over a mountain ridge, then sinks down again.

Westerlies Winds in mid-latitude regions that blow steadily – but often strongly – from west to east.

INDEX

A page number in **bold** refers to the main entry for that subject.

ACKNOWLEDGEMENTS

Dorling Kindersley would like to thank Lynn Bresler for proof-reading and the index; Christine Heilman for Americanization; and Dr. Olle Pellmyr for her yucca moth expertise.

Dorling Kindersley Ltd is not responsible and does not accept liability for the availability or content of any website other than its own, or for any exposure to offensive, harmful, or inaccurate material that may appear on the Internet. Dorling Kindersley Ltd will have no liability for any damage or loss caused by viruses that may be downloaded as a result of looking at and browsing the websites that it recommends. Dorling Kindersley downloadable images are the sole copyright of Dorling Kindersley Ltd, and may not be reproduced, stored, or transmitted in any form or by any means for any commercial or profit-related purpose without prior written permission of the copyright owner.

Picture Credits

The publisher would like to thank the following for their kind permission to reproduce their photographs:

Abbreviations key:

(Key: a-above; b-below/bottom; c-centre; f-far; l-left; r-right; t-top)

www.airphtona.com: Jim Wark 72bc; Alamy Images: Bryan and Cherry Alexander Photography 54bc, 71tl; Steve Bloom Images 11bl; Oote Boe 53cla; Gary Cook 29tr; Dalgleish Images 24bl; Danita Delimont 45bl; DIOMEDIA 21br; Terry Donnelly 67tc; Alberto Garcia 76-77b; Leslie Garland Picture Library 87tl; Robert Harding Picture Library 50bc, 51b; Colin Harris/LightTouch Images 21cr; David Hoffman Photo Library 83bl; ImageState 39bl; Justin Kase 35cla; David Noton / David Noton Photography 29tc; Dave Pattison 73crb; Chuck Pefley 13bl; Phototake Inc 86br; Ray Roberts 79bl; Jeff Smith 59tl; Joe Sohm 19br; Joseph Sohm 19br; Stock Connection 8br, 9tr; Stock Image 50bl; Homer Sykes 8cl; Tom Watson 54bl; Westend61 69br; Bryan and Cherry Alexander Photography: 27cra, 81tr; Frank Todd 18tl; Art Directors & TRIP: Helene Rogers 23br; www.atacamaphoto.com: Gerhard Hüdepohl 75b; © BBC 89cla; Michiel de Boer (http://epod.usra.edu): 55b; www.bridgeman.co.uk: 22cl;

Bruce Coleman Inc: J J Carton 18bl; JC Carton 18bl; Collections: David Mansell 25cr;

Corbis: Tony Arruza 51t; Craig Aurness 20tl; Steve Austin / Papilio 45br; B.S.P.I. 37cl; Anthony Bannister 75tr; Tom Bean 42bl; Steve Bein 27t; Bettmann 63tl; Jonathan Blair 48bl; Tibor Bognár 48br; Bruce Burkhardt 56bc; Chris Collins 23cr; Dean Conger 27crb; Chris Daniels 54t; Bernard and Catherine Desjeux 28tr; Warren Faidley 9b, 59br; Free Agents Limited 20bl; Alberto Garcia 76-77bc; Gustavo Gilabert 83cr; Farrell Grehan 15tl; Darrell Gulin 16br; Richard Hamilton Smith 89b; Henley & Savage 4-5; Walter Hodges 61cra; Hulton-Deutsch Collection 73br; Mark A. Johnson 73tr; Peter Johnson 78br; Wolfgang Kaehler 48-49t, 74c; LA Daily News/Gene Blevins 61crb; George D. Lepp 55tr; Massimo Listri 78bl; Grafton Marshall Smith 17tr; Rob Matheson 60r; John McAnulty 44bc; NASA 11br, 36t, 64bl; John Noble 68t; Charles O'Rear 75bla; Smiley N. Pool / Dallas Morning News 65r, 84bl; Clayton J. Price 15c; Jim Reed Photography 63b, 64tr, / Katherine Bay 61tl, / Jim Edds 87b; / Eric Nguyen 28bl; Roger Ressmeyer 33b, 83tl; Reuters 13tr, 62bl, 65cl, 70tl, bl, 75cr; Galen Rowell 25crb, 43tr, 49bc; Royalty-Free 34t; Ron Sanford 81cra; M.L. Sinibaldi 69t; Johnathan Smith / Cordaiy Photo Library 58cl; Paul A. Souders 28br, 73cra, 74b; Paul Steel 14b; Jim Sugar 83tr; Sandro Vannini 75cl; Michael S. Yamashita 59bl; Randy Wells 2; Anthony John West 43br; Staffan Widstrand 72tr; Zefa 46-47t; Empics Ltd: AP 9clb, 66t; PA 71cl; www.rfleet.clara.net: Richard Fleet 54br; FLPA - images of nature: B. Borrell Casals 61bl; Frans Lanting / Minden Pictures 80-81c; Steve McCutcheon 20br, 72bl; Flip de Nooyer 69bl; Getty Images: Adastra 23bl; AFP 71br; Altrendo 15tr; Daryl Balfour 19tr; Tom Bean 53r; Warren Bolster 35r; John Bracegirdle 30br; Per Breiehagen 73l; David Buffington 8cr; Gay Bumgarner 19bl; Chris Close 56br; Daniel J. Cox 41br; Grant Dixon 52b; Antony Edwards 37cra; John Elk 63tc; Michael Funk 53tl; Jeri Gleiter 53clb; Sean Gallup 84bla; Peter Hannert 37t; Pal Hermansen 68br; Jeff Hunter 58bl; Iconica 1; Johner Images 32l; Stephen Krasemann 60bl; Wilfried Krecichwost 83br; Frans Lemmens 80cl; Mike Magnuson 44bl; Eric Meola 40-41t, 62br; National Geographic / Michael Melford 26cr; John Miller / Robert Harding World Imagery 26cl; Alan R. Moller 58-59t; Pascal Perret 9tl; Per-Anders Pettersson 84tl; Photographers Choice 19bl; Photonica 35tl, 44-45t; Louie Psihoyos 81bc; Terie Rakke 53bl; Colin Raw 48c; Geoff Renner 25l; Nicolas Russell 83cl; Thad Samuels Abell Ii 50br; Joel Sartore 63tr; Philip Schermeister 80tl; Ed Simpson 11t; Jamey Stillings 33tr; Harald Sund 26b; Ken Tannenbam 57bc; Taxi 78t; Three Lions 71bl; Time Life Pictures 15b, 67b; Jean-Marc Truchet 8t, 21tr, 38br; Pete Turner 55c; Mark S. Wexler 77tr; Stephen Wilkes 50t; Ross Woodhall 17cl; Israelimages.com: Eyal Bartov 70bc; Hanan Isachar 70br; Kos Picture Source Ltd: 88t; Lonely Planet Images: Karen Trist 9ca;

Magnum: Ian Berry 37crb; Maya Goded 38bl; Gene E. Moore: (www.chaseday.com) 59cr; 62cl, c, cr; © 2004, Dr Alan Moorwood (amoor@eso.org) 55tc; Mountain Camera / John Cleare: 12t; Guy Cotler 12tr; N.H.P.A.: B & C Alexander 18c; Bryan & Cherry Alexander 18cla; Guy Edwards 18br; Haroldo Palo Jnr 43bl; NASA: 11c, 11fcr, 11cr, 12bl, 89clb, c, crb; NOAA 64br; National Gallery, London: 81crb; Nature Picture Library: Bristol City Museum 76bl; National Trust Photographic Library: John Hammond 22t; NOAA Photo Library: Ralph F. Kresge 47bra; NOAA Central Library, OAR/ERL/National Severe Storms Laboratory 87cr; Ocean-image.com/Mike Newman: 40c; Photolibrary.com: 24br; Diaphor La Phototheque 28crb; Paul Rapson (paul@rapson.co.uk): 86bl; Reuters: 59tr; Stefano Rellandini 52t; Andrew Winning 65bl; Rex Features: 70tr, 71tr; ESA 82bl, bcl, bcr, br; Keystone USA 84tc; Stuart Martin 35clb; SIPA 23bc, 82-83c;

Science & Society Picture Library: Science Museum Pictorial 42cl; Science Photo Library: Mike Boyatt / Agstock 45tr; British Antarctic Survey 49bl, 86tr; Dr Jeremy Burgess 39br; Peter Chadwick 29br; Georgette Douwma 13br; EFDA-JET 14tr; European Space Agency 87cl; FLPA / B. Borrell Casals 61bl; Simon Fraser 79t, 85b; Y. Hamel, Publiphoto Diffusion 76cl; Jan Hinsch 85cr; Adam Jones 46bl; John Mead 46bc, 57br; Peter Menzel 61tr, cl; NASA 10tl, 26tr, 42br, 67tr, 77cr; NOAA 79br; Pekka Parviainen 13cr, 47bl; Planetary Visions Ltd 61br, 66c;

George Post 49br; Philippe Psaila 86tl; Paul Rapson 51cr; Jim Reed 51c, 88bl; J.C. Revy 52c; David Scharf 76t; Mark A. Schneider 55tl; Peter Scoones 85tl; Sinclair Stammers 79cr; Alan Sirulnikoff 57br; University of Dundee 57tr;

US Geological Survey 11cl; South American Pictures: Tony Morrison 75tl; Still Pictures: A. Asad 67tl; Mark Edwards 77br; Martin Harvey 19crb; J.M. Labat / Bios 19cra; JM Labat 19cra; Ted Mead 38-39t; Tom Murphy 85tr; Gene Rhoden 84r; Francois Suchel 47tr; Superstock: Francisco Cruz 57tl;

TopFoto.co.uk: 77tl; © University Corporation for Atmospheric Research (UCAR): 59cl; Paul Watts / imageclick.co.uk: 27b; Weatherstock/Warren Faidley: 47br; Whiteplanes.com / Neil Stuart Lawson: 46br; http://sl.wikipedia.org: 34bl

All other images © Dorling Kindersley

For further information see: www.dkimages.com